Mule Deer Strategies

A HANDBOOK OF HUNTING TECHNIQUES

WALT PROTHERO

THE LYONS PRESS

First Lyons Press Edition: August 2000

Printed in Canada

10 9 8 7 6 5 4 3 2 1

Library of Congress Cataloging-in-Publication Data
is available on file.

Back cover photographs
Top: Outdoorsman's Edge President Markus Wilhelm
with trophy mule deer, photo credit/Peter Fiduccia
Bottom: Cary Dube of Beartrack Outfitters with trophy
mule deer, photo credit/Beartrack Outfitters

MULE DEER STRATEGIES

Acknowledgments

To Cheri Flory for paperwork and photographic assistance, and for encouragement and enthusiasm in writing this book, I owe more than I can say. Thanks also to my dad, Walter K. P., for getting me the illustrations for this book in such short order.

Thanks always to the good, fair foot-hunters I've shared camp-fires with, such as Myron and Wendell Powell (in the early days), Pete Spear, Bud Hendrickson, Charley and Herbie, and the rest too numerous to mention.

Thanks, too, to those rangers who were good enough to let me hunt on their grounds, especially Herschel ("Bud") Hendrickson and his wife, Martha, for always welcoming me, and to the Hadleys on either of their Wyoming ranches (and where I killed my biggest whitetail, but that's a story for another book).

And I owe a great deal to Mom, who in a fundamental way made this possible.

Foreword

My first mule deer hunt was in Crawford, Colorado, in 1972. (Which, as it turns out, is the same year that Doug Burris shot a monster mule deer in nearby Dolores County, Colorado, that still stands as the World Record.) I was slowly stalking the mountain rims high above the timberline. Every so often, I stopped to carefully glass the vast open parks, the shimmering stands of yellow aspen, the long, steep canyons, and the thick, black timber that dotted the landscape below. It was during the cool mid-morning, as the sun was just warming the hillside, when suddenly, a huge, non-typical mule deer buck exploded from an outcropping of rocks about 100 yards below me. Before I could gather my composure, the buck put another 300 yards between us. The terrain he covered while making his escape would have made a mountain goat choose a different route!

Only once, when he was at least 500 yards away, did he pause and look back in my direction. The buck stopped just long enough to let me get one last look at his magnificent antlers. As he stotted away over the backside of the ridge, I realized then and there that mule deer hunting was going to be much more challenging than I thought.

Since then, I've hunted mule deer throughout the Rocky Mountains. On each and every occasion, I learn something new about this diverse deer. The mule deer is, by necessity, a very cool customer—not prone to the instant panic attack of its cousin, the white-tailed deer. Mule deer, especially mature bucks, can and do endure some very tense situations from all types of predators— including hunters. Through it all, they have evolved as astute survivors.

To break through the mule deer's evolutionary defense system, hunters must have a wide-ranging arsenal of hunting tactics. This book covers a variety of strategies in exquisite detail. Strategies from rattling, stalking and stand hunting to tracking are all covered. This book is jam-packed with time-tested, solid advice from longtime pros who have successfully hunted trophy mule deer year after year. Featured sections include information for both novice and seasoned veterans to become better mule deer hunters.

Walt Prothero is a well-known hunting journalist and an authority on deer behavior and ecology. He has honed his hunting skills for more than thirty years during countless successful adventures. Much of the enlightening material in this book has been adapted from his articles that were originally published in *Field & Stream* and *Outdoor Life* magazines. The stories in this volume will enable any mule deer hunter to put meat in the freezer and a set of trophy antlers on the wall on his very next trip afield. This is the ultimate guide to more successful mule deer hunting—an absolute must-have for any deer hunter.

—Peter J. Fiduccia

Contents

MULE DEER STRATEGIES

1

Behavior, Ecology And
The Trophy Buck

The mule deer, like any other animal, is a product of its environment. Evolution within a range of habitat types had determined its behavior, physical attributes, food preferences and geographical distribution.

Behavior And Ecology

The most obvious difference between mule deer and other North American ruminants (animals that chew a cud and possess a complex digestive system) such as bison, sheep, pronghorn, goats, and other members of the deer family (elk, moose, caribou, whitetailed deer) is the size of the mule deer's ears in relation to the rest of the body. The size of the ear and its sound-gathering surface indicates the mule deer evolved in more open, probably drier country than, say, the whitetail. It also indicates the mule deer today relies on its ears as a means of detecting danger to a greater degree than the whitetail deer.

I have over the years walked very close to feeding whitetail deer. Several times I was unaware of the deer and not trying to be particularly quiet. One time sticks most vividly in my mind. I'd been out for two weeks on a backpack hunt for bighorn sheep in Montana, and I was returning to my truck along the Stillwater River. It had been a tough, unsuccessful hunt, and I was weary and in a hurry. I wasn't being at all quiet as I crashed through brush and slid down scree slides. I huffed and puffed up a rise along a canyon bottom and there, maybe fifteen yards away, a decent whitetail buck browsed completely unaware. I approached a few yards closer before he spotted me, then with a wave of his flag, disappeared into the timber.

That's only one instance, true, but it would never happen with a mule deer. Several times I've had muley bucks hear me hundreds of yards away, often after I'd made a relatively small noise. One buck I'd stalked in northern Utah heard the crack of a small branch I'd stepped on under several inches of wet, sound-muffling snow from at least two-hundred yards away.

Reliance On Eyesight

The mule deer also relies on eyesight more in detecting danger than any other North American game animal, with the exception of pronghorn antelope and mountain sheep, and in some situations, mountain goats—all of which normally inhabit more open country. Since the mule deer evolved and lives in more open areas than the whitetail, this makes sense. It also explains the mule deer's tendency to pause at the crest of a hill to look back at whatever frightened it. With today's adaptive mule deer, this trait is less prevalent than it was twenty years ago. Those bucks that displayed this "looking back" behavior were quickly culled from the population by armies of hunters now afield. Seldom, now, do I see a mature buck look back at danger.

The mule deer's sense of smell is probably as good as most other ruminants, though it doesn't seem to rely on it to the extent of those animals that keep to forests, like whitetails or moose. In the open country where mule deer evolved, scent was scattered by winds or disappeared because it was too arid. In my experience, mule deer are coming to rely more on scent. Very few bucks venture into open country during daylight hours; again, those that do are killed by hunters. Instead, they spend more of their time in thick timber and brush and as a consequence, rely more heavily on scent to detect danger, since by the time they see it in the close confines of a forest, it's too late.

Two Ways Of Running

Muleys run from danger in two ways: the most common is the stiff-legged trot; if the buck is really frightened, it bounds by striking all four feet together on the ground and driving forward and upward. These means of escape are products of the open, sometimes mountainous terrain where they evolved; they allow a buck to get over very uneven, rough terrain in a hurry, and they allow the muley to run with its head held high so it can watch for danger. The whitetail, on the other hand, is a more fluid runner, which allows it to snake under low branches or bound blowdowns without appreciably slowing down. Since the whitetail lives in more forested habitat, it can't see far ahead so there is no need for it to keep its head high to watch for danger.

Weight

As a rule, the mule deer weighs more than a whitetail. This isn't always true, however. Rue gives the average weight of a 4½-year-old Nebraska whitetail buck at 238 pounds; a mule deer buck at the same age averages 213 pounds. When whitetails do get heavier, it's in farm country. Here, whitetails are more adept at living in close proximity to man, and they make better use of farm crops. In the wild, though, mule deer are normally larger animals.

The first really big mule deer buck I killed—I was 14—field dressed at 268 pounds. I have since killed a number of bucks of from 220 to 244 pounds field-dressed (gutted); all had good, but not exceptional antlers. For what it's worth, the best trophy heads I've taken come from bucks that weighed between 195 and 220 pounds. One exception is a buck that field dressed well over 300 pounds that had an exceptionally heavy and even rack, and is one of the three best mule deer trophies I've ever taken. As a comparison, the heaviest whitetail buck I've killed, a good trophy with a total of 15 points, was killed on the Hadley Ranch in northeastern Wyoming and weighed 190 pounds after several days of drying.

Rutting Periods

Mule deer in the Rockies and more northern ranges rut, or breed, roughly from mid- or early November to mid-December. This leaves them at a survival disadvantage because they enter the tough northern winters in an often emaciated condition, and along with fawns who use ingested energy to grow rather than put on fat, are the first age/sex class to die in a moderate to hard winter. Typically, breeding bucks (not all muley bucks are) mature early, live hard, and die young. Mule deer seem to run themselves down to a much greater extent than do whitetails, too, another reason why the proportion of trophy mule deer is smaller than for whitetails. Southern desert mule deer rut about a month later, though I've seen them acting decidedly rutty as late as mid-February in Sonora, Mexico.

Fawns are born in late May or early June, a time of favorable weather, moist conditions, and good plant growth. Of course, since desert mule deer breed later, they drop fawns later, too.

Mature bucks in good vigor shed their antlers earliest after the rut, often within a month or so. They may shed them at the same time, or they may shed them several weeks apart. Antler growth begins to a small degree a short time after antler shedding, but the most rapid and marked growth occurs in June and July, a time of optimum, high-quality forage. Antler development depends largely on feed quality and quantity.

Descent From Summer Ranges

As a rule, mule deer begin to move down from higher summer and autumn ranges when snows of more than a foot accumulate. Usually, they follow natural drainages downward. Often, when this time coincides with deer season, trophy buck hunting can be astonishing.

I once caught such a downward migration in Utah. It had snowed heavily for a week in the mountains to the east of where I'd been hunting. All morning long deer wandered down the trail, down the finger ridges and slopes above. I must have seen a hundred deer before midday. Many were bucks and several were good, mature four-pointers (western count). By late afternoon I'd worked several miles up the canyon and climbed to a point above the valley floor where I had a good vantage point. Toward sunset, a good buck minced down the trail. I settled the crosshairs behind his shoulder, aimed a bit low to compensate for shooting downhill at a sharp angle, and squeezed. The buck gave a jump, trotted in a half circle, and collapsed. He had the best head I'd seen all day, but while I was dressing him, I glanced up the slope to where I'd been waiting, and just above stood two big bucks that dwarfed the one I'd killed.

Preferred Foods

Mule deer are ruminants, cud-chewers, and like cattle, elk, moose and others, have a four-chambered gut. This complex digestive system is needed to process coarse, low-quality feed. Ruminant digestion is an important survival strategy. It allows the animal to ingest large quantities of food in a short time, then retire to a secure hiding place, regurgitate the coarse vegetation, and rechew it (as a cud) before moving it down the digestive line. The ruminant, then, has to spend less time out in the open feeding where it is more vulnerable to predators like man.

Favored autumn and winter browse of the Rocky Mountain mule deer includes curlleaf and true mountain mahogany, bitterbrush, cliffrose, serviceberry, sagebrush, scrub oak (acorns and twigs) and any forbs that are left. In the summer, they normally feed on forbs and new shrub growth. Grasses and new forbs are used most in spring.

Distribution

Mule deer and its subspecies are distributed from the vicinity of the Great Slave Lake in northern Canada, south to central Mexico, and from Nebraska and the Dakotas on the east to the Pacific ocean on the west. They are found in the northern half of Baja, Mexico and a hundred miles south of the Arizona border. Sub-species of the mule deer include the desert mule deer of southern Arizona, southern New Mexico, eastern Texas, and south into western Mexico. Favored browse of desert mule deer include mesquite, creosote, rabbitbrush and the fruits of some cacti and acacia. As a rule, the desert mule deer runs a little smaller than its more northern cousin, though perhaps the biggest antlers are now coming out of Sonora, Mexico. This is keeping with Allen's Rule which states the farther north an animal lives, the larger its size. Moose are a good species to illustrate this: Shiras moose are the most southernly and the smallest of the moose varieties; next come the Canada moose, which lives farther north and is bigger. The Alaska-Yukon-Northwest Territory's moose is the giant and the one that lives farthest north. In spite of Allen's Rule, I've seen some titanic desert mule deer, mostly in southern Arizona and adjacent Mexico.

A few winters ago I was camping in Organ Pipe National Monument along the Mexican border in Arizona. I often make a trip there to break up the cabin fever of winter in the Utah Rockies, to hike, photograph, climb mountains, and watch birds and other wildlife. One evening, out on the flats away from the Ajo Mountains, I spied a truly big buck. He was with several does. His neck was swollen with rut. I stalked closer, hoping to get a good photo. I didn't get it, but I did get close enough to judge his size. His antlers were heavy, dark, and spread, I'd guess, about 34 inches. Quite probably he was sporting a record-class set of antlers. The following day I hiked to a remote valley and climbed a thorny hill to have a look around. As I walked around the curve of the slope, I jumped an immense buck that bounded over the top and down the other side. I ran to the top in time to see him standing in the ravine below. Through binoculars, I was certain he had a spread of 36 inches and heavy, high-reaching points. He'd score very high in the record book. He watched me a moment, then turned and trotted off through a *chollal*.

He was one of the two largest bucks I'd ever seen. It's hard to guess his weight, but he was as big as the average trophy buck up north.

The mule deer evolved in brushlands and open forests. Barriers to distribution would be areas devoid of these habitats, in other words, unbroken climax conifer forests, level woodlands, or prairies devoid of brush. The Great Plains were effective barriers to distribution eastward. Even if mule deer did somehow manage to migrate past the Plains, the closed woodlands would have been unfavorable for survival. As a result, the mule deer is a western animal.

Habitats—The Edge Effect

The mule deer inhabits a variety of habitats within the western part of the continent. Mule deer are found in bare, volcanic mountains in northern Mexico, to rolling grasslands with woody or brush draws in southern Arizona and New Mexico, to open lodgepole pine forests in Montana, to alpine basins in much of the Rocky Mountains. One necessity of all these habitat types is plenty of "edge effect." The "edge effect" is a term used in wildlife management, and it states that whenever two types of habitat comes together (for example, a stand of timber and an open, grassy park), the edge between the two types will be more favorable than either type alone. Both the number of species and the total bio-mass (weight of living organisms) will be greater in the edge area than any comparable area located wholly within one type or the other. Typical edge areas in the Rocky Mountain states include the division between stands of scrub oak and sagebrush communities, between aspen and spruce forests and brushlands, between conifer forests and sagebrush or grasslands, and between pinon-juniper forests and brushland. I'd guess 95 % of the deer I've killed have been in such places.

The "edge effect" is obvious to anyone that's spent much time in the wilds, though perhaps they haven't thought of it in such terms. Large, uniform forest seems almost lifeless. After hiking through such an area, one is amazed at the abundance and variety of wildlife around an open meadow.

The Trophy Buck

Antler Size

The size of a mule deer's dichotomous (double forking from the main beam, as opposed to whitetailed deer, who have only a single forking) antlers is influenced by the age of the buck, its health, its diet, and heredity. Some studies indicate that the shape and number of points on a mature buck is influenced most strongly by heredity, while the size of antlers is a result of diet. Soil type plays a big part in the amount and what nutrients accumulate in feed plants, and consequently in the growth of antlers. Since most antler material is composed of calcium and phosphorous, soils rich in these elements produce the biggest antlers. Limestone soils produce, typically, big antlers, and these are plentiful in the west. You can determine what soils an area has by looking at the record books, either those of the Safari Club International, or of the Boone and Crockett Club. It's a safe bet that areas that produce trophy heads also have soils high in calcium and phosphorous.

Obviously, a buck needs time to produce good antlers. Even in good soil areas, a buck is seldom a trophy before 4½ years of age. Most trophy bucks are from 5½ to 10½ years old. After that, antlers get smaller, spindlier, and produce fewer points. The age when trophy quality decreases depends on the buck and its health and heredity. If hunting pressure is too heavy or too efficient (an increase in gadgetry often increases efficiency, or at least the percentage of bucks harvested), bucks are killed off more rapidly at younger ages and don't get time to grow to trophy proportions. As a result, these days, there are simply fewer big bucks to go around. Half-a-dozen ranchers I know in several states state that fewer big bucks show up now on winter range. Many places that were noted for trophies in the sixties now produce nothing bigger than a young three- or four-pointer. What few mature bucks do survive, spend a higher proportion of time in timber or thick brush, become nocturnal, and often retreat to isolated areas during hunting season. If you want to kill a trophy buck these days, you've got to take these into account.

As an example, back in the sixties I'd get a trophy buck every year in northern Utah, typically around the magical 30-inch spread mark. Now, I'll see one that big only every six or seven years, if that often. Hunter pressure has increased five-fold in Utah where I hunt, since the sixties. The same thing is happening elsewhere—in western Colorado, parts of Wyoming and Montana. But probably nowhere has the trophy buck hunting plummeted to such an extent as in Utah, where for too many years the game agency (they seem to change their name every few years; I think they're now calling themselves the Division of Natural Resources) sold tags to whoever wanted one and they were good for virtually every area in the state. Where about every male over the age of 14 can and does hunt deer, and in a state that has a birth rate equivalent to many third world countries, buck hunting has to suffer. There is some glimmer of hope, however; Utah now has drawings in some areas, has shortened the hunting season, and adopted other conservation practices that should improve trophy buck hunting.

Hopefully, It's Not Too Late

Hunters won't see positive results for years, yet. Other states, particularly Wyoming, Idaho and Nevada, have initiated conservation practices some years back which are gradually improving trophy mule deer hunting. It seems Utah took longer to take positive action, probably because the tremendous revenues generated by unrestricted license sales were too big of an incentive to accept things as they were.

Considerations For Antler Judging

Considerations for judging trophy mule deer antlers includes the spread, both inside and outside, length of the main beam, length of the points, number of points, heaviness, and in my estimation, some intangibles such as general configuration. According to the Boone and Crockett Club's system, consideration is given to inside spread (distance on the inside between the main beams at the widest point), length of main beam, length of points, heaviness, and evenness. The range of inside spreads as listed in the 8th edition (1981—sorry I don't have a more up-to-date copy) *Records of North American Big Game,* range from $19\,^3/_8$ to $31\,^6/_8$ inches in the typical category. The greatest inside spread of any buck I've taken is just under 29 inches. The length of the main beam is measured from the base along the outside to the tip of the first or anterior point, and in The Book, it ranges from 22 to just over 31 inches. One of my heads measures 28 inches. The circumference measured between the antler burr and brow tine ranges from $4\,^2/_8$ to $6\,^5/_8$ inches; I've got one that goes $6\,^4/_8$ inches. Whether or not one approves of any kind of "mine is bigger than yours" competition in hunting, the parameters set up for trophy judging, either by the Boone and Crockett Club or Safari Club International, seem to be the standards by which trophies are judged. The difference between the B&C system and the SCI system is that almost any mature animal will be listed in the SCI book. In a way, that reduces shenanigans in the SCI system, since most hunters get their names listed without doing anything illegal, such as poaching, buying or stealing big trophies, "doctoring" trophies to make them larger, shooting animals in national parks, and whatever else one can and has done to get a head in the B & C book.

More trophy bucks have come from western Colorado, specifically Montrose and Mesa Counties, than anyplace else. According to my 1981 edition of the *Records of North American Big Game,* the world-record typical mule deer was bagged in Dolores County, Colorado, by Doug Burris, Jr., in 1972. According to several accounts of the hunt, Burris didn't just luck into the animal; he's a real hunter—thorough and experienced. I'd wager most "Book" heads were taken simply by bumping into them, lucky in other words.

Mule deer antlers are larger and more impressive than whitetail antlers. Whitetail antlers differ from muley antlers in that all tines on a typical head branch from the main beam. For years, mule deer antlers have been classified by how many points there were on one antler, excluding the brow tine. A typical mature buck was usually a "four-pointer." Yearlings normally had "two points." The Eastern Count takes in the total number of points on both antlers, including brow tines; it was used mainly with whitetail deer. A typical mature four-point mule deer buck (western count) was actually a ten-point buck by eastern standards. Eastern count includes all points, including brow tines, and is really a better way to judge trophies. More westerners are going to the eastern system, or to a system that tells the number of points on each antler, such as 5 x 5, etc.

To be a little redundant, in order to produce trophy antlers, a buck needs three things: (1) time to get large—most trophy bucks are 5½ to 10½ years old; (2) proper genetics—the buck must have inherited some pre-disposition toward large antlers; (3) good feed from country that hasn't been overgrazed by livestock and from mineral-rich soils. If you find a place with all three of the above, you're fortunate indeed, and then you can worry about trophy judgment in the field.

Judging Antler Spread In The Field

To no hunter's surprise, judging a trophy that lies at your feet or one hanging on the wall is a world simpler than judging one bounding off through the aspens two hundred yards away. Arguably the best way to judge mule deer trophies in the bush is to compare the spread of antlers to the spread between the ear tips. For many years I've read, and accepted, that the spread between ear tips on a big mule deer buck was about 18-inches. I finally got around to actually measuring the ear tip spread, and was astonished to find that

18-inches is too low. Like many, maybe most, old wives' tales, this one didn't stand up to scrutiny. Every adult buck I measured, and the number must be over 50, had an ear tip spread of from 20 to 23 inches. Therefore, if antlers seem to spread about ("about" is as close as you're going to get in the field) 4 inches beyond the ear tips on either side, that buck will have an antler spread around 30 inches. If the antlers seem to spread six inches beyond ear tips, you've got a whopper between 32 and 35 inches, so don't let him get away.

For too many years, I believed the 18-inch figure, and I used it to judge trophies in the field. I remember one good buck I shot in the mid-sixties. I'd been hunting all week and passed up a number of bucks. Time was running out, and I had only a few days to hunt before returning to college classes. I was working down a canyon in the dusk when I spotted a buck on a rimrock high above. Even at four- or five-hundred yards, I could see the big spread. I stalked closer, found an aspen with a fork at just the right height, rested my rifle in it, and tried to judge the buck. He was staring hard, and through the scope, screwed up to 9x, I saw his antlers spread four inches or so beyond each ear. Given the 18-inch between-the-eartip spread, that buck would only have an antler spread of 26 or 28 inches. Still, I had the impression the buck was bigger. Since I hadn't had much luck getting a buck, I squeezed off. The first shot hit a bit far back and the buck wobbled for cover; the second shot hit the heart and the buck collapsed a few feet from thick brush. When I got to the buck, I was amazed. He had the widest spread of any buck I'd killed to that point. Just the same, his antlers didn't spread much beyond 4 inches over the ear tip spread. Later, I measured the antler outside spread at just over 32 inches, an exceptional trophy, and his ears spread 22 inches, tip-to-tip.

Antler heaviness and height are also good parameters for quick judging a trophy buck in the field. The only real way to get good at judging trophy mule deer in the wild is to compare heads, and probably the best way to do that is to compare mounted heads.

All this aside, what makes one buck a trophy and the next one not, is in the eyes of the hunter. If you're happy with the buck, value it for some reason, and not only based on size, that animal is your trophy. It doesn't matter that the buck won't even make the SCI Book, let alone the B & C Book. To the old buck hunters who remember the golden years of mule deer hunting back in the sixties or beyond, a trophy is most often any buck around 30 inches in spread. Today, a 30-inch mule deer is comparable to 65-inch Alaskan moose, a 17-inch pronghorn, a 10-inch mountain goat, or a 7x7 bull elk. In other words, it's one of the toughest animals to collect in North America. But don't let someone else's judgment of trophies color your judgments; anything is a trophy if you think it is.

For *me,* a good trophy mule deer is a fully mature buck with big antlers for the country, no matter if they make anyone's record book.

Doe browsing on sagebrush—a mule deer staple, especially in winter. *(Courtesy of Cheri Flory.)*

Buck nipping dried forbs. *(Courtesy of Cheri Flory.)*

2

Six Methods For Mule Deer Hunting

Some hunters, or even guides, may be good at only one or two kinds of hunting—standing or driving for instance—and never try anything else. That would be all right if those methods always worked, but sooner or later, they're going to fail.

A good example of this kind of inflexibility occurred just last November when I was hunting whitetails with an outfitter in western Saskatchewan. The outfitter relied mainly on stand-hunting and driving to collect bucks. On my six-day hunt, I was able to rattle in two small bucks from my tree stand but had seen no adults. The other three hunters had even less luck. On the other hand, we quite frequently found big tracks after a fresh snow, but the guides just didn't think tracking would be fruitful. They'd apparently never tried it, or if they had, it hadn't worked. I'd had great luck at tracking, not only for whitetails, but also for elk, moose and especially mule deer. I'm still convinced that if I'd been left to my own devices, I'd have tracked down a good whitetail.

Year after year, a friend of mine uses a good stand overlooking a major escape trail that runs from a canyon, through a saddle and into a very rough gorge where big mule deer apparently hide during hunting season. He's more often than not successful, and he's taken some good bucks from that place. But if he doesn't get a buck on opening day, his chances drop 90 percent. If he hasn't taken one by the second day of the season, odds are he won't at all, because the majority of the bucks that are going to be pushed through that trail have already been pushed. Before long, he simply gives up. If he felt more comfortable with stillhunting and tracking, for example, he could hunt into that gorge and have a good chance of getting a buck.

The hunter who is adaptable, on the other hand, and who can use all mule deer hunting methods with nearly equal facility, is the guy who constantly brings home an animal with good antlers. If you're caught in a hunting rut and have only mediocre success, try the following mule deer methods. You'll

27

become a "complete" mule deer hunter, and you'll probably be happy with the results.

Stand-Hunting

Site Selection

Stand-hunting for mule deer, though not quite as popular as stand-hunting for whitetails, is the most popular method of hunting in many places. Most mule deer stand-hunters aren't as sophisticated as their whitetail counterparts and understand little about the art of stand selection.

The most common error muley stand-hunters make in selecting a site is finding one that looks good to them, not necessarily to the deer. The trick is to select a stand that will afford a high probability of seeing deer, not one that's out of the wind or against a sunny warm stump. Trails between bedding and feeding areas are very good bets, but first a hunter has to find one. Typically, big mule deer bucks bed in thick timber or brush and feed in open areas not far from bedding sites. They use one to four trails to go to and from feeding areas, and even if there is more than one trail, more often than not one will be more heavily used than the others. It's a good idea to determine when a given trail is used—often a big buck will leave the timber on one trail in the evening to feed and return to it on a different path in the morning to bed. So you'll need to wait along different trails in the morning and at dusk.

Always situate your stand downwind of the feeding or bedding trail you're watching, of course. When the air is cold, it typically drifts downhill, so if you're watching in the cool evening near sundown, or in the dawn before sun-up, hide downhill of the trail. There are enough variations to that rule, especially in the mountains, to make doing some research on your own prudent.

As my opening-weekend buddy has found out, standing along escape trails can at times provide exceptional action. Escape trails, obviously, are trails deer use to run from danger. They usually, though not always, lead to places where deer will be relatively safe, such as a vast and thick stand of timber or brush, inaccessible gorges or swamps. One advantage of ambushing along escape trails is that bucks are often so intent on escaping they're less alert to danger ahead. Select a stand that is downwind and out of sight. Logically, these escape-trail stands are only useful when other hunters are in the vicinity and moving deer.

I've got a favorite place on the rim of a large canyon in northern Utah where I like to just sit and stare out over a vast chunk of wild, spectacular country, especially after things have begun to settle down after the opening-weekend melee. By midweek, most hunters have left the hills and deer are starting to get back into at least some of their routines again, and often deer have been pushed into the canyon by crowds in other places. I've seen more than 40 deer at a time from the boulder where I usually sit. And I've made a number of stalks after I've found a good buck.

Several seasons ago I spotted a fair buck probably three-quarters-mile away. I eased down through the thick Douglas fir timber below me, stalked quietly through the willows and chokecherries and across a beaver dam in the bottom, then made my way up and into an open, sagebrush-covered slope. The buck was browsing just over the ridge, across the ravine. I stalked carefully across the crest, hidden by some big fir trees, and then down into the timber. I spotted the buck from an opening. He was just across the small creek, browsing in a thicket of wild rose and oblivious to anything but sweet rose hips. The light was fading quickly, and I could just barely make out the crosshairs as I settled them behind his shoulder. I pressed the trigger and the muzzle flash blinded me momentarily. When I could see again in the near darkness, the buck was gone, but I'd noted a single spruce near where the buck had been browsing. It was fully dark by the time I made it to the tree, and when I walked in the direction where I'd last seen the buck, I tripped over him. He hadn't moved a step.

Stillhunting

My favorite method of big-buck hunting is stillhunting. When you're stillhunting you drift through woods and openings, looking ahead and listening carefully, searching for something that doesn't quite belong. You move slowly, and try not to miss what's there. The idea is to find a good buck before he sees you and runs.

It's best to stillhunt into the wind, of course, but it's also possible to do it when the wind is from the side, or even when it's behind you. Strong wind directions aren't as critical because any scent is scattered far and wide. Hunting in a strong or moderate wind is also good because it masks any sounds you might make, and it's often possible to get quite close to bucks. One disadvantage of stillhunting in strong winds is that it makes big bucks even more spooky.

Stillhunting in thick timber is an exciting proposition. Any game you find is going to be close, so you must shoot quickly. Chances are that about the time you make out a bedded or hiding buck, he'll see you and run for it.

Actually, stillhunting in timber is often a combination not only of still-hunting, but of tracking and stalking as well. It's important to stillhunt more slowly and quietly than you would in the open. When you encounter the deer they are apt to be much closer, and mule deer have not only incredibly keen hearing (witness the large ears), they have a sense of smell that under the right conditions can pick up a man at a mile and eyes nearly as acute as those of pronghorns.

In western Wyoming some years back, I spent much of one cold November chasing a buck around and through an extensive, two-mile-long stand of lodgepole pines. One morning I was moving along a well-used game trail through the timber—there were elk, moose and deer tracks on it. I knew from previous observations that the big boy I'd been hunting used it to travel to one of his favorite feeding areas.

It had become almost second nature for me to watch on the downwind side of any trail, because typically that's where big bucks will bed and where they can get a good scent and watch their backtrail. I had much more than the normal amount of anticipation that morning as I stillhunted. I was sure that something would happen. I'd been easing along the path for more than an hour, watching, listening and even smelling. With the wind in my face, twice I'd caught the heavy, musky scent of bull elk. Twice I thought I heard the "roar" of a rutting muley buck, but the sound was so faint I couldn't be sure. As I eased around the curve of the slope, I caught a faint movement out of the corner of my eye. Then I saw antlers above a deadfall, but they weren't big enough to belong to the buck I'd been after. I heard a roaring grunt from just up the slope, and a big buck rushed down at the smaller one. My .270 was up as he trotted and bounded down the loose, pine-needle duff hill, leaving big dark slashes in the soil. As he cleared a thick growth of saplings, I pressed the trigger quickly before he could disappear in timber. The monster buck skidded down the slope on his nose. Two does I hadn't seen and the smaller buck crashed off through the forest.

Driving

Driving, or pushing, is a common tactic to whitetail hunters. It's not quite as common in mule deer country, but it is used and it can be effective. Basically, driving mule deer, like any other species, involves pushing game past the hunters in your party who are posted ahead of the drive near likely escape routes. Good places to post hunters in mule deer habitat include canyon or ravine heads, river-bottom goosenecks, and river or brush "islands." Driving can be good in any weather, though unfortunately, a drive may frighten an old buck right out of the area for the duration of the hunting season.

A good tactic is to post hunters at the head of a canyon, forming a half-circle around it, with hunters stationed down the side slopes a few hundred yards. Then, drivers, whether on horseback or afoot, push up-canyon.

For years, a troop of horseback hunters drove a big canyon that I frequently hunted. Hunters were posted at the head of the canyon and in the saddle that led into another canyon. The horsebackers started a mile or so below and pushed up the canyon bottom and side slopes toward the shooters waiting above. There was always a good deal of shooting, but most of the bucks they collected were small. There was a side ravine thick with brush and timber part way up the canyon, and I often posted myself along it during the drive. I must have done it at least five times, unknown to the drivers, and I collected two good bucks there.

Decent buck and early snow.

Another good place to drive is on river-bottom goosenecks or peninsulas. Rivers in the West turn frequently on themselves and create small or large peninsulas up and down a river bottom. The best way to drive these peninsulas is to position "sitters" across the river from the peninsula tip, and then drive from the base of the peninsula toward the top. Deer will often break from the sides of the peninsula and cross the river, but drivers can usually hear them splashing and make it to the riverbank as the buck climbs out on the other side. Or, the deer will bound out of cover at the peninsula tip and hesitate before entering the water, and this provides the hunters on the riverbanks an excellent shot.

A third good place to employ driving is on river or brush islands. The techniques used are similar for either. Quite frequently, there are stands of timber or brush surrounded by relatively open country. These islands often contain bucks. This is a fairly simple drive—the island is surrounded by hunters, and a driver or two is sent into the tangle to push deer into the open.

Brushing

Brushing, at least how we define it where I come from, is similar to driving except it's not necessary to post sitters. In other words, one person can do it, and the object is to move deer to a place where you can get a shot, such as an open slope of a canyon or ravine.

The Stop-Pause-Start Technique.

One brushing method I use is what I call the stop-pause-start technique. A hunter works up a likely canyon or ravine preferably above timber or brush, or on the open slope, finds a likely looking place to stop (perhaps to eat lunch), and after 20 or 30 minutes, he starts out again. Often if there's a buck in the vicinity, he gets pretty nervous while you're just sitting there. When you start out again, he's about convinced himself he's been spotted, and he'll flush.

A few seasons back I'd picked a large south-facing slope of a plateau to brush later in the hunt, perhaps after bucks from other places had been pushed into it. There were a number of ravines running off the plateau. The southwest-facing slopes were pretty open, covered with only a few stands of short, twisted oak scrub, chokecherry or maples. The southeast-facing slopes had more brush—mostly stands of bigtooth maple and some larger stands of oak.

I hiked up one steep ravine on the brushy southeast-facing slope, hoping to flush a buck from the brush below me onto the opposite open slope where I could get a shot, but it didn't exactly work that way. I sat down directly across a ravine from a big, short tangle of oak brush. It was a nice day, so I had lunch and enjoyed the sun beating down on me. I lingered a bit as my mind wandered here and there. Probably a half-hour later I stood up, fumbled around for a few moments, and started off up-canyon again. At that moment, a good buck bolted from the oak brush just across the ravine and started bounding up the open slope. I was so startled I missed with the first shot, but then I cooled out and drilled him between the shoulder blades. He was a good fat four-point buck (10-point Eastern count).

Platoon Brushing

Another method used frequently in the West is what I call"platoon brushing." It's used by platoons of horseback hunters. They simply ride through brush and hope to flush deer onto the opposite slope of the canyon where they can get some shooting. Too often, though, the shooting is hurried and deer are wounded and it spoils the day for other foot hunters in the area. I don't encourage this type of brushing.

One of the simplest and most effective methods of brushing out muleys is to move up a canyon on the timbered or brushy north or east-facing slope, with the hopes of flushing bucks from the timber below to the open opposite slope. This has been an effective technique for me for years though now it's less effective for really big bucks. The trophies that survive today's crowds are smarter and less apt to run from the brush until they're absolutely certain they've been detected.

Tracking

Tracking is one of the most satisfying methods of collecting a trophy. It requires patience, finesse, intelligence and a certain single-mindedness. You have to always be aware of wind direction, where you put your feet, and the habits of big bucks (which are quite different from those of younger bucks).

Four years ago I spent the better part of three days tracking a huge buck I'd spotted the day before the season opened. His trail led in and out of canyons, through stands of timber and brush, across creeks and boulder slides, over ridges and plateaus, and into a completely different major river drainage.

I learned a lot of things on that trail, among which was what a big buck's hoofprint looks like (a good fore track measures about 3½ inches long); where bucks bed (most often where they can see and smell their backtrail); what they feed on (there, at that season, it was bitterbrush, wild rose, cliffrose and a variety of dried forbs); what times of day they tend to move during hunting season (mostly at night); and how to find a track again after I'd lost it on hard clay or rocky ground (by making ever-widening circles until I found the print again on soft soil). In the end the tracks moved into a steep, rough canyon and the droppings were fresh again. As I moved in, I spooked him from a chokecherry thicket below, and three days of tension were suddenly released. I was astounded by his size, and I cleanly missed with the first shot. Again, I settled down and I hit him twice with fatal shots.

The Loop Method

A common tracking technique is the "loop method." It's been used for millennia by primitive hunters not only on this continent, but any place where man has hunted big game. When using this method, the hunter finds a set of tracks he wants to follow and follows them directly for a short distance. When he's got an idea where the buck is going, he loops on the downwind side of the trail, returning to it every few hundred yards if it's in the open, or every 50 or so if it's in heavy brush. Because big bucks habitually bed downwind of their backtrail, chances are the buck won't scent the hunter using the loop method because he's downwind of the trail most of the time, too. If the hunter passes the end of the trail, he makes smaller loops back in the direction where he last saw the tracks. The shooting is often done quickly because the buck is apt to be surprised at close range.

Rattling

Rattling for whitetails has been written about for a least a century, and recently it's been refined almost to the point of being a science. Mule deer rattling, because it's not nearly as successful or as well-known, has received almost no press. Granted, it's not as fruitful a method as it is for whitetails, moose or even elk (yes, I've rattled in all of those species), but it can be useful during the rut, when a number of does are in estrus in a given area at a given time. It may also work very near the center areas of a big buck's home range, especially just before the rut. If other methods aren't working for you at these times, try rattling. It may just put the venison in the freezer, as it's done for me.

When I took my first mule deer using this method, rattling was just a novelty for me. Earlier that morning I had found a buck that had died earlier in the autumn. I broke his antlers from the skull and put them into my daypack. Toward evening I stillhunted through a stand of spruce, found several big rubs in proximity to several beds (which indicated I was in the muley center, or core, area). What the heck I thought, and quietly took the antlers out of the pack. I clattered them together, waited a few minutes, and clattered them again. I heard the unmistakable grunting roar of an irate, dominant buck just upslope, and a moment later he crashed down through the trees. If I hadn't shot him when I did, I think he may very well have run over me. And I got him because when other, more common hunting methods failed, I was able to reach into my bag of hunting tricks for one last technique.

The most complete mule deer trophy hunter, and the most successful one, is going to be the guy who can use all methods, and whatever else is necessary, when combing muley country. To be successful, he's got to be as adaptable as his cagey prey.

3

"Run" And "Hide" Muleys

Back in the early '70s, when I was conducting my research on elk behavior for a graduate degree in wildlife biology, I ran into more than a few big mule deer bucks. Though my primary concern was with elk behavior, I couldn't help but become distracted by the huge bucks I'd sometimes see in the high Absarokas just north of Yellowstone, in Yellowstone itself, and in northern Utah. Before anything else, I was a deer hunter, so I started taking notes. After a few years of this, I began to realize that behaviorally, there were basically two kinds of bucks. One would rely on running to escape, the other would rely on hiding. Often, there would be bucks of each type on the same mountain.

Since then, I've kept notes on the types of bucks taken by hunters. Whenever a big buck was killed, I'd try to find out exactly how it happened. What I've noticed is a new pattern in the behavior of big bucks. Most would rather hide to avoid detection than run to escape danger. This is even more true in heavily hunted areas, with some places inhabited almost exclusively by deer that are hiders. Only in remote country, such as the Beartooth-Absaroka Wilderness in Montana and various areas in central and northern British Columbia, will deer still run from what they perceive as potential danger. With today's flat-shooting rifles and superior scopes, the runners are the first to get killed off. The bucks that survive are deer that have been raised by does that tend to hide in response to human activity, or ones that learned early in life that it's safest to hide when hunters are about. Back in the '60s, the golden age of mule deer hunting in Utah where I learned to hunt, it seemed that the big bucks I took were all runners.

Runners

I believe that the natural tendency for mule deer—ones that haven't been hunted extensively—is to run from approaching danger. Then they'll stop, if in the open, and watch their backtrail to make sure that the danger is far enough behind. If it continues to threaten them, they'll run some more. With their ground-eating bound, trot, flat-out run and endurance, they were pretty safe from all predators from mountain lions to primitive man. Then came the rifle, and soon the methods of escape that evolved over millions of years were no longer effective. Before mule deer had time to adapt to this new threat, they'd gained the reputation of being the whitetail's retarded cousin. Now that they are adapting, they are finally being regarded as an intelligent and desirable trophy. There are still places where big bucks can be taken almost as they were more than 25 years ago when I began hunting in the now-overpopulated country of Weber County. Mule deer still stand and gawk at hunters across a canyon in the wilderness of British Columbia, in the Sun River country and in the Beartooth-Absaroka Wilderness of Montana.

Hunting in such areas is mostly a matter of getting out early when bucks are feeding in the open, or again late in the afternoon or early evening. Brushing them out into the open where the hunter can get a shot is another good technique. It's a joy to hunt bucks like this. Little hunting pressure means lots of runners, and you can daydream about how all mule deer hunting used to be.

Hunting runners is simply an easier proposition than hunting the hiders, at least if you're somewhat of a marksman. The most common and easiest method to flush out runners is to simply sidehill up a canyon with the idea of flushing deer onto the opposite slope where you can get a shot. Back in the '60s, this was about the only technique I used. I'd simply work up-canyon on one of the side slopes, preferably the one with more brush or timber, with the idea of spooking deer out of the brush below and up onto the relatively open south or west-facing slope. The shots are often long, 200 or 300 yards, but if the slope is open you may have time for several shots if you muff the first.

One of the runners I recently killed—which scored 201 Boone and Crockett Club points—was taken using this method. I'd seen the buck that day before the opening of the season as he made his way up through a stand of fir and aspen. It was the eve of deer season, and the buck knew it—he'd heard the parade of four-wheelers and all-terrain vehicles on the road two miles to the north and was moving to a safer place. I picked up his tracks the next morning and stayed with them for the better part of the following three days, returning to camp each night exhausted from the hiking and concentration. It was the longest I'd ever tracked anything. On the afternoon of the third day, as I was slowly following the tracks down into a steep, rugged canyon, I got a very strange feeling. I'd had the feeling before, so I knew better than to try and discount it. The best way I can describe it is as a feeling of anticipation—action-to-come. I moved up the canyon on the side slope, above the tracks in case he'd circled above his backtrail. A small four-point flushed from a patch of oak scrub and bounded into the canyon bottom and up the opposite slope. A bit farther on, a forkhorn and a doe repeated the maneuver. I continued up the canyon when suddenly the big buck flushed from somewhere down the slope, bounded the stream, and made his way up the opposite side. Three days of tension burst like a balloon. I was so excited that I missed clean with the first shot. On the second, I settled into that quiet, impersonal state you shoot from when you do it right. Like a wild bronc just out of the chute, the buck lowered his head and kicked with his hind legs. I knew that he was already dead, but I was taking no chances. I held ahead and a little above as he trotted across the slope, and hit him again. I wouldn't be surprised if he was the last trophy-size runner I'll take out of that country.

Hiders

If you're hunting country that isn't true wilderness, as most of us are forced to do these days, adult bucks will typically be hiders. Don't waste time waiting for a trophy buck to feed out of a stand of timber into the open and then expect a nice, open broadside shot. It just doesn't happen that way much anymore. You may catch small bucks that way, or see does and fawns, but unless it happens to be during the rut, the big bucks are going to stay hidden and won't move during the daylight unless you just about step on them. Because the majority of hunting seasons occur before the rut, hunting trophy bucks means flushing them out of their beds and taking a quick shot, usually at close range.

Hiders behave more like whitetails, elk in timber, or even black bears. Hiders will most often stay close to heavy brush or timber. When they do, they are difficult to approach. Mule deer bucks have perhaps the keenest hearing of any game on the continent—and can smell at least as well as whitetails or elk. And they rely more heavily on eyesight. In other words, they're darn tough to stalk once they have bedded. It requires the stealth and silence of a leopard, the patience of Job, and the reflexes and shooting eye of Billy the Kid. In addition, hiders will not, as a rule, flush until they are absolutely certain they've been detected. They've learned that most humans can't find them if they lie absolutely still. Probably the best way to find hiders is to track them.

One season, I would consistently find large deer tracks in an open flat on a plateau. The flat was full of good deer feed—frost-dried forbs, wild rose, cliff rose, mahogany and sagebrush—but in spite of my dawn-to-dark vigils, I couldn't catch a glimpse of the buck. He would only feed at night, then return to the timber before first light. After about three days of waiting, I decided to follow his tracks down into the thick spruce and fir of the north-facing slope of a large canyon. Unfortunately, the tracks were heading downwind so if I stayed on his trail, he'd eventually smell me before I could get a shot. At that point in my hunting career, I'd already learned that under such situations, it was best to make loops on the downwind side of the trail, returning to it every 100 yards or so to make sure that I hadn't overshot the end of the trail. If I did overshoot it, I'd make smaller loops back in the direction of where I'd last seen the tracks. I also knew that typically, smart old bucks make a buttonhook on the downside of their trails when they bed so that they can smell, and usually see, their backtrail. I'd made several loops downwind of the trail as I moved along in the direction the buck had taken. I kept my rifle ready and my thumb on the safety because if I got a shot, it would have to be taken quickly. I moved slowly and quietly, keeping close watch on where I put my feet, and straining to see as far ahead into the gloom of timber as possible. I hadn't gone 200 yards into the timber when I saw something that didn't quite fit. I stared at it for several minutes. It seemed to be a large, dark knothole on a weathered deadfall that lay in a tangle of broken branches. It was just 30 feet ahead, and I stared at it for what seemed like hours. Then it blinked! At exactly that instant, the rifle came up and my thumb flicked off the safety. The buck was up and over a log as I fired. A few hairs drifted away in the breeze. The buck was a good one and very fat.

Sometimes, you'll find a hider on a relatively open slope, ridge or meadow. But they'll behave the same as one in thick brush. They won't move until they're sure they've been spotted.

I hunted a particular buck for four straight seasons. The buck had a variety of tricks in his bag, and most of the time they worked on me or other hunters. Once, I had located the buck on an open slope across a wide canyon. He was bedded in a scrubby clump of maples and was too far away for a shot. One-quarter mile down the canyon, four hunters on horseback were heading straight for him. I was sure that they were about to kill "my" buck. I thought briefly of opening fire or shouting to scare the deer out of the country, but I figured that it would be unsporting. It probably wouldn't have worked anyway. The horsemen came on: 200 yards, 100, 50, 20. The buck had stretched out his neck and lay his head along the ground. Two horsemen rode above the clump of maples and two below, not 30 feet from the buck. He didn't move. When the hunters were far enough up the canyon to no longer pose a threat, I stood up. I'd reasoned that if the buck had let them pass so close without moving, he'd let me, too. And I knew where he was. But the moment I stood up, the buck saw me and stood up himself. Somehow he'd known that I'd detected him, and he trotted up the slope and over the ridge. Several years later I did manage to collect the buck, but that's another story.

Sometimes, bucks may hide in places where you wouldn't think there was enough cover to conceal a fair-size prairie dog.

Once, my longtime hunting buddy Rick Lovell, a heavyweight wingshot, and I were hunting sage grouse across the top of a flat plateau in Weber County, Utah. The tallest vegetation on the plateau was shin-high stunted sagebrush. Much of it was little more than ankle-deep. We were working toward a small wind-tortured knee-high clump of fir. At the most, we had maybe expected to flush some grouse from the scrub, but were startled nearly out of our shoes when a big buck bounced out and took off for the next canyon. He'd let us approach to within 20 or 25 feet.

Another time, in Wyoming's Red Desert, I was making a stalk on a nice antelope buck. He had a large harem, so I was stalking not just one pair of eyes but 25. I was on my belly and squirming my way up the last few yards of the rise where I could get a shot. I eased into a small gully, not even the size of a small irrigation ditch, when I came face to face with a good mule deer buck 15 feet away. We scared the pants off each other and he, not content with startling me out of five years of my life, also frightened off my antelope. He'd been hiding in a small depression where the scanty vegetation was scarcely a foot high.

There seems to be fewer good bucks in country that gets moderate-to-heavy hunting pressure. This only makes sense, because even hiders aren't invulnerable and the more hunters in a given area, the greater the odds that someone will stumble onto a good buck and collect him. So make sure that there are some good bucks in the country you're hunting.

The only way to do this is by pre-season scouting. If there aren't any runners around, you have to look for tracks. An adult buck's track is unlike the track of either a small buck or a doe. The hoofs of a big buck point outward somewhat, especially if he's just meandering along, as he'll almost always do unless he's frightened or after a doe. A large buck will usually leave drag marks between prints when he's ambling along in soft soil or snow, just as a fat man is more apt to shuffle than a lean, energetic younger man. Aside from track size, a big buck will sink more deeply in soft soil. The best way to learn to recognize deer tracks made by different age- and sex-classes is to observe them during the summer. Because there are no hunters afield then, even big, old hiders are apt to revert back to their running behavior. Note where a big buck has walked, and then go and look at his tracks. How do they differ from those of the forkhorn you tracked?

Now that you know what a big buck's track looks like, see if you can find any in the area you are going to hunt. Don't do your scouting too far in advance of the hunt because changing seasons produce changes in feed plants, and bucks that were there in September may not be there in October. I usually do most of my scouting a week or so before the season opens.

Mule deer have changed since the day of the runners. They'll hide until they're nearly stepped on. Last season in western Colorado, I watched a group of hunters work up the canyon from the river bottoms of the Dolores River, pushing bucks as they came. Smaller bucks and does streamed up the trail just below where I was perched on a sandstone rimrock. Apparently, the hunters were inexperienced, because they'd posted no one above to intercept anything that might flush. One hunter was passing a small clump of tall sagebrush a few yards below me. I thought I saw something move in the sagebrush and put the glasses on it. It was a good buck, with a total of 11 points. He was standing and moving around some tall sagebrush to keep it between himself and the hunter. The hunter passed on by and moved up the canyon. Before long, another hunter walked by the sagebrush on the other side. The buck repeated the maneuver, then lay back down. I had my camera and managed to get a few photos of the maneuvering. After photographing and watching the buck, I didn't quite have the heart to shoot him.

Later in the day, I shot a small buck, dressed and dragged him toward the sagebrush where the big buck was hiding. I then sat at the edge of the sagebrush not 15 feet from him. It was several minutes before that buck flushed and bounded down into the canyon bottom and up the other side. The last I saw of him, he was topping out onto a timbered mesa. I guess he'll very likely die of old age.

My good friend Richard Lovell and my jeep full of bucks.
The big one on the right is mine and spreads 32 inches.

4

Big Bucks I've Hunted

The big muley buck had simply vanished. Earlier, watching from a canyon to the east, I had seen the buck come off a high ridge and into the wide, bare, rolling draw where the only cover was sagebrush. Now, on the lip of the draw, I scanned slowly with binoculars.

The sun had set some time ago and frost was settling on the tawny grasses and blue-gray sagebrush. The light was fading fast. I shrugged and walked back up the ridge toward the truck. On the ridge, I scanned the draw one more time. The buck was in the bottom! He was stretching like a big dog, rump in the air and forefeet extended in front. I was too far away for a shot and, by the time I worked close enough, it would be dark. The big buck had been there all the time, lying in the short, 20-inch sagebrush, watching me. Looking at him through the binoculars, I could have sworn he was grinning.

That was only one of several hundred encounters I have had with big muley bucks. He was one of the many that got away. I have hunted deer for 30-odd years in five Western states. I've bagged more than 60 good bucks. In these hunts, I've run across some pretty unusual bucks—smart, equipped with incredible patience and steady nerves and, above all, unpredictable.

The Sheepherd Buck

Perhaps the smartest buck I have ever hunted was the one I named the "Sheepherd Buck." He lived in the canyons draining into Sheepherd Canyon in northeastern Utah. I hunted this buck for four consecutive seasons. Each year, I saw the buck at least once and usually twice. Each time, I got a chance and each time—except the last time—I was outsmarted.

One time, early in the deer season, I came upon the buck in a thick growth of maples. I could see him sneaking away. I ran to the opposite slope of the small draw and watched. Nothing happened. After awhile, I walked back to the maples and picked up the buck's tracks.

43

He had crossed the ridge beneath two big spruce trees, the only place he could have gotten out of the draw without me seeing him. I followed the tracks. In the next canyon, he had joined up with five other bucks. As I crossed the ridge, I saw the bucks silhouetted against the snow in thick maples on the opposite slope.

Five bucks were browsing unaware. The sixth deer, the Sheepherd Buck, was watching me. I moved down the slope toward the bucks, using the scrub oak for cover, but I didn't fool the big one. He continued staring. One by one, the other bucks picked me out. They were within rifle range but in thick brush. The big buck had gotten behind the other deer. Then they ran, slowly at first, then more quickly as they became panicked. The Sheepherd Buck kept the other deer between himself and me.

Just before the fleeing bucks were about to cross an opening, the Sheepherd Buck took off at a right angle and ran up through the thickest brush on the hillside, zigzagging from one stand to the next. The last I saw of him that year, he was crossing the ridgeline 600 yards away.

Another time, while watching some horseback hunters who were "brushing" the opposite slope of a canyon more than 500 yards away, I again saw the buck perform some incredible feats of patience and intelligence. He lay in a tangle of maple and willow while three horseback hunters passed within 10 yards. After they passed, he stood up and slowly and deliberately walked up the slope. He laid down in a clump of willow. A few hundred yards below, more hunters were riding up the canyon. They rode right through the place where the old buck had been bedded earlier. After they had passed, the buck stood up and casually walked down to his first resting place.

On opening day of the following deer season, I got into the buck's favorite draw across from his favorite stand of maples, long before daylight. I sat on the opposite slope. As the light began to come I saw a buck disappearing into the brush. Was he the Sheepherd Buck? I waited. Big, heavy clouds raced by from the northwest. Finally, I moved down into the draw and circled around the growth of trees. For some reason, just before moving down into the maples I looked back across the draw to the place where I had been. A few feet from where I had been sitting, the Sheepherd Buck stood. He twitched his tail and walked over the ridge. I guess he figured the safest place to be was the one I had just come from.

There were other adventures with the Sheepherd Buck, and most of them made me the dunce of the encounter, but the big buck finally made a mistake. He was getting old, I knew, and his antlers were a little smaller than they had been the year before. I saw the buck standing in a small clump of brush on the opposite slope. He was staring down toward the lower end of the canyon. Hunters were coming up the bottom a thousand yards away from him. The Sheepherd Buck stared in the direction of the noises and perhaps his preoccupation with the advancing hunters was the reason why he did not detect me. I was a long rifle shot away, but I didn't want to shoot into the brush. Then the buck stepped into an opening, perhaps trying to better sense the oncoming danger below. I settled the crosshairs of the .270 at the top of his shoulder and squeezed. The buck leaped at the shot and came down a few yards lower on the slope. He didn't seem to be hit, and he had located me. I raised the crosshairs to a few inches above the top of the buck's shoulder and squeezed again. This time the buck jumped into the air and came down running. I was sure I heard the bullet strike flesh. He ran into some brush and then tried to make it over the ridge. He died trying. The 130-grain bullet had taken him through the heart. The buck had a 33-inch spread and very high-reaching antlers.

A Buck In Nevada's Ruby Range

A buck I once killed in Nevada's Ruby Range perhaps best illustrates a muley buck's steely nerves. I camped in my pickup beside a small stream at the base of a long, bare slope that led to a ridge. The ridge, in turn, led to some steep canyons and jagged peaks to the south. A little farther than midway up the slope, in a slight depression, was a small, thick tangle of willows and aspens that was perhaps 15 yards across and maybe 20 long. Surrounding the tangle was open slope, grass, and wind-stunted sagebrush—nothing over 10 inches in height.

I had been hunting for more than a week and had seen only does and small bucks. Each morning, I walked by the patch of brush on the hillside on my way to the ridgetop and the canyons to the south. I often walked next to the brush and I always passed within 10 or 15 yards of it.

One afternoon, on my way back to camp, I stopped a few yards from the patch of brush to enjoy the panorama of the valley below. The aspen and cottonwood leaves were like phosphorescent gold in the afternoon sun. Sitting slightly above the patch of brush, I idly tossed rocks into the aspens and willows. I had tossed a half-dozen stones when an incredible commotion broke out. The tops of several 20-foot saplings swayed violently, brush popped, and then an immense buck broke out of the other side of the growth. I was so startled, I fired the first shot in the air. He headed across the slope with all the speed he could muster. A bullet caught him in the back of the neck as he was disappearing over the curve of the slope.

Later, I checked the tangle of brush in detail. The buck had been staying in the patch. The whole interior was trampled with big deer tracks. Willows had been heavily barked by antler polishing. There was a small water seep near the center of the tangle. Several of the rocks I had tossed were lying on the main bed. Perhaps I had hit the buck with one of them. From all of the sign in the patch of brush, it seemed the buck had been there all the time. I had passed within a few yards of him every day.

Hunting At Utah's Causey Reservoir

One summer, not too long ago, I was able to find time to fish the upper reaches of Causey Reservoir in northern Utah nearly every evening. I would paddle my canoe the four or five miles to the back of the rugged, steep-sided reservoir and fish until dark. A big buck lived in a small draw high up a steep, brush slope broken by gray, limestone cliffs. I saw him browsing on cliff rose and mountain mahogany nearly every evening. He was there through August, September, and early October. (The Utah deer season opens in the last half of October.) I figured I had a sure thing. I even made wagers on it, but I lost. The buck had somehow sensed the advent of deer season, perhaps because of the appearance of hunters and the sounds they made, perhaps simply because of the time of year. The buck disappeared several days before the season opened. I hunted hard but I didn't see him.

In early November, a week or so after the deer season had closed, I paddled the canoe up the reservoir to have a last try at the browns that were still spawning in the feeder creeks. Looking up the slope toward the big buck's haunt, more out of habit than anything else, I was pleased to see the old deer. He was feeding on the slope just as he had during the summer and early autumn. I have had similar experiences with other muley bucks. Maybe they become nocturnal in their movements, or maybe they move to rugged or inaccessible areas come hunting season. It's probably a combination of the two.

One summer, I made several backpacking trips onto Buffalo Plateau in southern Montana's Absaroka Mountains to scout for elk. During that time, I found a monster buck that hung out in the rocky ridges at the end of Elk

Creek Basin. I was sure the buck would make the record book. I saw him a number of times that summer, always within one-quarter mile of the ridgetop. I packed in two weeks before the opening of elk and deer season to scout and enjoy the Indian summer weather. The buck was still there, and there were several bull elk in a basin to the south. Things looked good.

As opening day approached, outfitters began moving hunters into and through the country. The buck just disappeared. I shot a nice bull elk, packed him out to the truck and horse trailer 20 miles to the north, and headed home to Utah.

I drove home through the northern part of Yellowstone National Park, actually only seven or eight miles from where I had been hunting though more than 100 miles by road. In Yellowstone, next to the highway near Tower Junction, I saw the buck. He was being photographed by several tourists as he browsed. He had not gotten big by being a dummy. There was no mistaking the buck. He had five long, heavy points on each side and his antlers were perfectly matched. He was the largest buck I had ever seen, and I'm sure he would make the top 10 in the record book.

The Buck With The Sheep

One deer season about 12 years ago, I came across a buck with very unusual habits. During the summer, I had heard about a big buck that hung out with a herd of sheep. I didn't put much stock in the story, though.

That deer season was hot and dry. I hunted hard but hadn't seen one decent buck and only a few small ones. Each evening, I hunted a small draw in the head of Utah's Magpie Canyon. Over the years, the place had consistently yielded good bucks, and I'd always seen deer there. One evening, I reached the ridgetop and peered over. The draw was full of noisy, smelly sheep. The herders were moving their flocks out of the mountains for the winter. I stood up and cussed, pondering my next move. Then I saw a tawny flash in the brush below and, a moment later, a great buck bounded up the opposite slope. I dropped to a sitting position and fired at the buck. The first shot grazed his neck; the second entered between the shoulder blades and exited through the brisket. The buck fell three feet from several sheep. He had jumped up within less than 10 feet of several others. Later, I talked with the herders.

"Sure," one said in heavy Basque accent, "he been with the sheep all summer."

I had never believed any self-respecting buck would even be in the same canyon with sheep, let alone travel with them. And because many hunters don't believe it either, that's probably the reason he survived so long.

The Buck From The Hidden Hollow

Even more unusual was the buck I hunted during the 1981 season. I had set up camp on a ridge overlooking the North Fork of the Narrows of the Ogden River in northern Utah. The country is rugged—steep canyons feed into the headwaters of the Ogden River, which flows in a steep limestone gorge 1,000 feet below. Because of its ruggedness, the place gets little hunting pressure.

I scouted the country several days before the opener. The weather had been perfect—mild days and cold, crisp nights. I had seen a number of deer from camp through the spotting scope. One was a good buck. I saw him near a peculiar, orange, sandstone cliff. At the base of the cliff grew a huge, old Douglas fir. Surrounding it was a thick growth of scrub oak.

Opening morning found me across the draw from the orange cliff. I was within easy rifle range of the place where I had seen the buck. After watching for a while to no avail, I crossed the draw and checked out the rock. There were large, fresh deer tracks. I felt sure they had been made that morning— probably before light—but there was no sign of a deer bed. A ledge crossed the face of the cliff 20 feet up. I moved out of the brush and back across the draw. The big Douglas fir covered much of the face of the cliff but, from what I could see, it looked as if the ledge crossed from one side to the other. I hunted back toward camp and had lunch.

I watched the ridges and canyons from camp with the spotting scope that evening. Just before dark, the big buck was again feeding at the base of the orange cliff. One moment, there was nothing; the next, as if by magic, there was the big buck. It was as if he could appear and disappear at will. I hunted back to the orange cliff in the morning. Still no buck. I couldn't figure it out.

I clawed through thick oak brush to the ledge. There were big tracks on the ledge. I eased along the ledge and sat down next to a large, cavelike hollow. There was a sudden, loud, shrill, whistling snort and a flash of gray rocketed past me and over the ledge. The buck landed in the scrub oak 20 feet below and crashed down the draw. I was so startled, I nearly fell off the cliff. I never did get a shot at the buck. From across the draw or from camp with the spotting scope, I couldn't see the hollow because it was hidden behind the fir.

On the last day of deer season, I again approached the cliff. I was on top of it and began dropping stones onto the ledge below, hoping to spook the buck out. I dropped several stones before I heard a movement in the brush above and behind me. I turned just in time to see the buck disappearing over the ridge. For all I know, that buck still roams the rugged canyons above the Narrows of the Ogden River.

The intelligence of big whitetail bucks is legendary. But the whitetail is more predictable; the muley buck is apt to do anything. Where the whitetail is high-strung and spooky, a big muley has nerves of steel and seldom panics. The only rule that works in hunting big mule deer bucks is to be ready for anything.

5

Combing A Canyon
For Mule Deer

Along with "antlers make poor soup" and other bits of deer-hunting wisdom that were popular when I was learning the sport, I was told that I'd become a "sidehill galoot" from hunting the canyons too much. According to the theory, I'd wear one leg shorter than the other on the slopes and, as an old sheepherder friend told me, "you'll walk in circles on the flats." Well, I've been hunting canyons for more than a score of years now, and though some of my friends might argue that I've spent more than my fair share of time going in circles, my legs are still pretty much the same length. And I've learned that while you can't quite make soup of antlers, you can make a pretty passable margarine-like spread by boiling them. So much for old stories.

Pushing

There are basically three strategies used when walking a canyon for mule deer. The first is to push deer into places where you can get a shot. Most mule deer country is arid, much of it to the point of being desert. As a result, the north- and east-facing slopes, which get less direct sunlight in the Northern Hemisphere and hold more moisture, are normally the slopes that are forested. South- and west-facing slopes are usually pretty open, growing sagebrush, grasses, and a variety of short brush. When you walk a canyon, the objective is to push deer off the timbered or brushy north- and east-facing slopes onto the open south- and west-facing slopes where you can get a shot.

When you use this strategy, it is important not to panic the deer into an all-out running escape, or you'll soon discover the difficulty of hitting a bouncing buck fleeing across a canyon 200 to 300 hundred yards away. Move slowly and quietly into the timber. Mule deer have perhaps the keenest hearing of any game animal on the continent—witness the large ears—so they'll

50

A hunter moves through ravine-bottom brush,
periodically climbing onto a sidehill to scan ahead and across.

eventually detect you if you're just walking normally. Then usually they'll move off at their own pace, hoping that they haven't yet been spotted.

When moving through a stand of timber or heavy brush with the intent of pushing a buck onto the opposite open slope, be aware of any openings on your side. Remember, you have to shoot out of the cover across the canyon. Hunt through the bush from opening to opening, glassing the opposing slope repeatedly. If openings are hard to find, return to the ridge periodically for a better vantage point.

Sometimes stands of timber or brush are small enough that you can get deer moving simply by letting them catch your scent. Early in the morning and after sunset, the air is cold and dense in most locales, and it usually flows downhill. Get above the trees during these time periods, and let your scent drift to the deer. If you have a strong feeling about the place, don't be afraid to wait; it may take awhile for a buck to move out from scent alone. During daylight hours, as the air becomes warmer and less dense, it usually moves uphill. In that case, get below the timber, but watch the heads of the canyon or ravine. In a very small patch of cover, throw rocks long enough for deer to get nervous. Once in Nevada's Ruby Mountains, I tossed rocks into a growth of willows about the size of a large living room. I threw six or eight, and then waited—not really expecting anything to hide in such a place, since it was in the center of a completely open slope. I chucked one last rock and heard a peculiar thunk. In the next moment a huge buck crashed out of the willows as if the hounds of hell were after him. I was so rattled that I missed with the first two shots, but managed to collect him with the third.

If letting your scent drift into the patch and tossing rocks into it doesn't work, walk through it. Large bucks will frequently lie in brush until they're absolutely sure they've been detected. If a deer is jumped that way, it'll waste no time leaving the country. Be ready.

In a small canyon with shallow slopes it's often necessary to make only one pass through the timber. It's best to start at the head of the canyon or ravine and work downhill. That way, it is less likely that you'll lose deer out of the head of the ravine or gully. When you have made it to the bottom of the main canyon, move up across the open slope and repeat the procedure.

In a small canyon with steep slopes, the stands of cover are apt to be larger, since the slopes receive less direct sunlight and lose less moisture to evaporation. In such cases it is best to work slowly through the timber several times.

In large canyons (defined for our purposes as a canyon too large to shoot across from rim to rim), hunt it in sections. Work each part as a separate canyon. In all likelihood there will be small, shallow side canyons and/or small, steep-sloped side canyons. There will also be larger stands of timber.

Stillhunting And Tracking

In large parcels of timber, it's best to still-hunt and track on the upper slope of the stand. Concentrate your still-hunting efforts along deer trails. Move upwind along the trail if possible, and be aware that trophy bucks typically make a buttonhook downwind of their backtrail and bed where they can scent and usually see any approaching danger. In such cases, identify the downwind side of that route and focus your attention there. If the downwind side is indiscernible, watch off to both sides and as far ahead as possible. Any shooting under these conditions is apt to be quick and at close range, so keep the gun ready, just as you would when approaching a shorthair on point.

When tracking a buck, more often than not he will make things difficult for you by moving downwind, rather than upwind. If that is the case, make loops downwind of the trail, returning to it every 100 yards or so. If you move carefully enough, you might catch him in his bed downwind of his backtrail. This, too, may require fast shooting.

Ambushing

Pushing (or starting) and still-hunting and tracking in timber are best during daylight hours after deer have bedded down. A third method of canyon hunting is best as early in the morning or as late in the evening as possible. This is done by simply moving to places where you're most likely to see deer. Unlike pushing, the idea is not to be detected.

Since open slopes are where deer predominantly feed, they are good places to catch deer early, before they have returned to bedding areas, and late, after they've left beds. Slopes where deer have been feeding are best identified by tracks—the more the better. Also, look closely for cropped twigs (the older the cut, the browner, more oxidized it will be), forbs, and small plants that have been pulled up. It's also useful to be able to identify browse plants, which include bitterbrush, mountain mahogany, cliffrose, wild rose, chokecherry, sagebrush, and others. Mule deer also feed on a variety of dried forbs in the fall, as well as on the seed heads of certain grasses. Some open slopes, for one reason or another—usually relating to poor soil quality—may actually support little deer feed, while an open slope in the next canyon might be thick with it. Since early and late is prime-time hunting, don't bother with slopes that grow little browse.

Trails to and from bedding and feeding areas are good bets early and late. These, too, are easy to identify—just look for a concentration of tracks. Most deer bed in heavy cover during the day, so expect them to be moving into timber with advancing light. As a rule, the largest bucks will bed earliest in the morning and come out of timber to feed after dark. It's best to keep an eye on trails where they leave or disappear into cover. It's not uncommon for deer to use one trail to leave timber and another to enter it, so read the tracks.

Prime muley real estate is found in Utah, Nevada, and parts of Arizona, New Mexico, Montana, Idaho, and in western Wyoming and Colorado. But mule deer also inhabit marginal range, such as extensive forest areas on the west slope of the divide in Montana and British Columbia, and in northern Idaho. Canyon hunting in these areas is mostly a matter of still-hunting or tracking, or maybe waiting along the edges of old burns or clearcuts.

Typically, I'll use all three methods—pushing or starting, still-hunting and tracking, and ambushing—when hunting any given canyon. It's mostly a matter of choosing which method to use where.

Maybe the old sheepherder was right when he told me I'd become a "sidehill galoot" if I hunted canyons too much. But as far as I can tell, my legs are still the same length and I don't exactly walk in circles on the flats. I do feel out of place there, however, and I'll make a beeline for the nearest canyon every time.

When combing a canyon for bucks, you sometimes can get this close.

6

Bucks At The Edge

I had as much sensed as actually seen the buck against the gray oak scrub. The sun had set and I had been still-hunting down the canyon toward the stand of oak brush and the opening where I'd seen a buck with a wide-spreading rack the evening before. It was really asking too much to expect to see the buck again, I told myself, so I wouldn't be too disappointed if he wasn't there.

Small bucks and does were feeding out of the dense stands of timber and oak as the evening came. I put the glasses on the deer. It was him, all right. He was standing at the edge of the oaks, cautiously looking out over the clearing. I crawled through the sagebrush to a small aspen with a fork at just the right height. The buck was staring hard in my direction as I took off my jacket and stuffed it into the fork, then lay the rifle across it. The buck had taken a step down the slope, as if to see better, and was very interested in what was going on on my side of the canyon. When the crosshairs were just behind the buck's shoulder, I squeezed the trigger. He turned on wobbly legs for the oak brush. I led him a bit and squeezed again. This time the buck dropped, only a foot from cover.

His antlers measured 32 inches. He was the first buck I'd taken with a spread greater than the magical 30 inches.

At that point in my hunting career, I had no concept of what "edge" was and had never heard of the "edge effect." I'd killed several bucks in earlier years and would kill more before I found out about "edge." In spite of my ignorance, most of the deer I'd take would be found in the openings near large stands of timber, oak or aspen, like that big buck.

The "edge effect" refers to the fact that whenever two habitat types come together, the edge between them will be better as habitat than either type alone. In the West, I have taken many more deer in the edge areas between conifers and sagebrush than I have in the sagebrush or timber alone. The same is true for oak-grasslands, aspen-shrub, or other such communities.

Actually, the edge effect is apparent to anyone who has spent much time hunting mule deer. Extensive uniform forests seem almost lifeless. After hunting through such an area, one is amazed at the abundance of life—not only of deer, but of birds, rodents, elk, and predators along a thicket, meadow, or old burn. Large bucks these days bed in the thickest timber or brush they can find, but it is hard to sneak up on them. Most deer, including trophy bucks, are seen as they leave or return to timber along the edge of a grassland or short-brush community where they can get good feed and are only a jump from safety.

The largest buck I've ever taken was never seen more than a step or two from cover. One reason was safety. The other was because the buck couldn't get high-quality browse—bitterbrush, mountain mahogany, cliffrose, and forbs—in the thick stands of maple or oak where he usually bedded. Every time I saw the buck in the ten or twelve encounters I had with him, he was never more than two hops from a thick stand of trees. Some of his companions, younger bucks who were not yet schooled in the ways of men, would often stray farther from cover. Chances were, though, that these bucks would never reach his age.

The day I finally bagged the buck, he was standing at the edge of a thick and extensive stand of big-toothed maples. It was his favorite haunt, and I'd seen him there several times. I was lucky that day. I put the crosshairs at the top of his shoulder and squeezed the trigger. At the shot, the buck gave a great leap down the slope and landed a few yards into the maples, miraculously in a small opening between trees. I raised the crosshairs a few inches higher and squeezed the trigger again. The deer bucked heavily, and a moment later the sound of the bullet striking floated across the canyon to where I was sitting in the snow. The buck ran off through the bare maples before he fell.

One way to hunt the edge is to locate a good buck, either by tracks or previous sightings, and just wait for the buck to come out into the open. If the buck is large, old, and smart, a hunter may have to wait for several days to catch him as he comes out just before dark or returns at first light.

I used to regularly hunt the mountains east of Cokeville, Wyoming. At the head of a small but steep ravine there, bucks would often come out of a dense stand of aspen and lodgepole pine to browse along the "edge" of the open sagebrush. Almost every evening I would see bucks; and often enough to keep it interesting, a fair-sized four-point or two would show up. It was November, and by sundown the temperature was usually not far above zero. I timed my hunting so I would not get to the head of the ravine until nearly dark. It was sheer torture to stay still for any length of time in the bitter cold. By the time I'd arrive each evening, the cold, dense air was draining rapidly down the ravine, into my face and away from where I hoped the big buck would appear. I knew there was a good buck around; I'd seen tracks so large a mouse would have a hard time getting out if he ever fell in one.

I'd been hunting five or six days, arriving at the ravine just before dark. I'd about made up my mind to take the next four-point that showed itself. I'd been camping in a small tent, and the weather was cold—seldom getting above 10 degrees during the day. I was just about worn out from hiking and trying to stay warm. I wanted to go home and sleep in a warm bed.

As I peeked over the rim of the ravine, there were several deer scattered about the sagebrush near the edge of the aspen. One was a smallish four-point (ten-point Eastern count). They were completely unaware of me. I had the crosshairs behind the buck's shoulders for a moment before deciding to wait. The buck wasn't going anywhere, and there was still some shooting light left. I could always collect the little buck at the last moment. At that instant a larger four-point walked out of the aspen and started browsing in the sagebrush. Then another, even larger buck appeared. Then the third and largest buck stepped into the open. He was no 30-incher, to be sure, but he was the best buck I'd seen on the hunt. He dropped without a quiver at the shot. The other bucks disappeared into the aspen as if they were smoke.

Another method of hunting the edge—one more suited to my restless temperament—is to still-hunt. I like to sneak along just inside the cover of trees with the wind in my face, or at least close to it. This method is particularly effective where a stand of timber meets a grassland or shortbrush community. I know of just one such spot in southwestern Montana. Lodgepole pines sweep down from the top of a plateau to the east. At the edge of the pines, where most of the deer bed, grows a grass/forb/shrub community. Apparently there are several browse plants there that deer love. Small bucks and does are found along the "edge" between the two communities as early as mid-afternoon, and often all day if it is very cold or if a storm has just moved through. The adult bucks, however, do not appear until just before dark, if not later.

Walking just inside the timber is easy and, due to the thick carpet of pine needles, very quiet. If he is a little careful, even a novice hunter can sneak up on deer with that setup. I had been walking slowly along the edge of the timber all afternoon and had covered perhaps 2 miles. I'd jumped a score of deer, and could have bagged several small bucks, though none was larger than a forkhorn. I'd spent most of the hunt searching for a trophy, without luck, and now my time was running out. I needed a nice fat buck for the freezer.

At one place, where a peninsula of timber, maybe 100 yards wide at its base, pushed into the sea of tawny autumn grasses, were a number of does browsing placidly a few yards from the edge of the timber. The sun had just set and it was getting cold. A coyote wailed from somewhere out in the open brushland. I moved carefully through the trees, just screened from the deer, then through the heavy timber of the peninsula toward where it ended in the grass and shrubs. As I neared the end of the pine-tree peninsula, deer were suddenly bounding in every direction. I vaulted a blowdown and ran to the edge of the trees. A dozen deer were trotting across the open area, back toward the timber I had just come through. The last was a decent buck so I swung just in front of his shoulders and squeezed the trigger. He dropped at the shot, struggled a moment, and lay still.

One of my favorite methods of hunting is to glass distant slopes. In the morning deer, and for that matter, elk and moose, are feeding along the edges of distant stands of timber, aspen, oak, or maples. Before long they will disappear into the security of the trees. In the evenings, deer come out of the trees and browse along the edge between the two plant communities. It is not uncommon in wild country, especially if it is late in the season and the weather is cold, to see several hundred deer in a evening's glassing. If a big buck is located, a hunter can plan to be there at first light, or at least by the following evening.

Several times while hunting in northern Utah I had seen a good buck feed out of a stand of spruce and fir on the other side of a gorge. At first light one morning, I was in the bottom of the canyon below the big buck's stand of timber. Bitterbrush, mountain mahogany, a few clumps of cliffrose, as well as a scattering of frost-dried forbs, all favorite deer browse, grew along the mostly open slope. There were large deer tracks and fresh droppings. I paused to catch my breath and stare out over the big canyon. Suddenly I had the feeling I was not alone. I looked over my shoulder and standing just at the edge of the timber was the big buck. He whirled and disappeared into the shadow. I didn't even have time to bring the rifle up. Ironically, a year later, at first light, I killed a six-point bull elk at that very spot.

Artificially created edge is as attractive to deer as the natural variety. I frequently hunt on one or another of Bud and Martha Hendrickson's ranches in western Colorado. Most of the natural vegetation along the Dolores River consists of pinon pine, oak, juniper, and a scattering of grasses and other shrubby vegetation. One of the best places to see deer is at the edge of the large alfalfa fields spread along the creek bottoms.

One evening just before last deer season, Bud, my hunting companion Rick Lovell, and I drove around some of the fields to check on deer and the deer-frightening devices, (which were actually a string of firecrackers contributed by the game department and designed to ignite every few minutes and scare the deer from the alfalfa). The alfalfa fields were surrounded by a mixed stand of oakbrush and pinon pine and they were irregular in shape, following the contours of the narrow redrock canyons. Deer were everywhere. In the space of a few hours we spotlighted somewhere in the neighborhood of 700 deer. Eighty to ninety of these were bucks. A few of them were four-points of three or four years. Probably there were a few real mosshorns around, but they were smart enough to head for the rimrocks when they heard our pickup. The deer-frighteners were having no effect at all. Possibly the deer even liked them.

The situation was ideal. There was plenty of edge and the deer were staying in the vicinity. In one direction was the cover of oak and pinon, as well as acorn and pinenut mast, and in the other was succulent, nutritious alfalfa. It was a bit like a deer Garden of Eden. I was after a trophy buck, so I wandered the high rimrocks. Unfortunately I didn't find a good buck, so on my last day I decided to hunt along an alfalfa field. Rick had already bagged his buck as it left the alfalfa, so he accompanied me on the final afternoon of our hunt.

We were walking along the edge of a pinon-juniper forest a few yards from where it bordered a large alfalfa field. We hadn't gone 50 yards when I saw a deer lying under a pinon tree across a tiny ravine. It was a buck and he hadn't seen us. In fact, he was sound asleep. At the shot, he simply stretched out his neck and lay still. He was a small four-point; no trophy, but a fine piece of meat.

Man seems as instinctively drawn to the edge as mule deer, elk, or moose. Most hunters don't like to camp in heavy timber, probably reasoning that it's too gloomy or closed-in. Few like to make camp in a vast, open prairie. They feel, I think, too vulnerable to the elements. Perhaps another reason hunters prefer to make camp along the edge is that the place looks like game country.

By limiting himself to the place where two major plant communities meet, a hunter can make his hunting time more productive. If he concentrates on the edge areas and forgets both the large, uniform forests and extensive open areas such as prairies, he increases his chances of being in the right place at the right time.

To me, the edge means big-game country. It is an unmistakable feeling. When I move into a long canyon where the black-green timber is fringed by tawny grasses and blue-gray sage, something in me tightens. I check the rifle, scan the canyon, and move slowly into the wind. I'm ready.

Dried forbs and other good deer feed grow
at the "edge" between two plant communities.

7

Muleys In Timber

"Look at that!" my hunting partner said. He was looking across the plateau at a huge buck that had just come out of a ravine less than 100 yards away. The buck stood in the sagebrush and stared at us for a moment as I brought the jeep to a halt. We watched the buck as he trotted across the open flat and then across the four-wheel-drive trail in front of us. Then, he went down into the aspens on the northern slope of the plateau. We had both killed bucks earlier, so we couldn't shoot. I like to think we wouldn't have done so, anyway. It seems less than sporting to shoot a deer so close to the car.

That was the last really big buck I've seen out in the open during the season. The year was 1972, if memory serves. These days, big bucks just aren't seen in open country when hunters are about. The bucks that do show themselves never grow to trophy proportions. Bucks that live long enough to have a good head do so by becoming survival experts. And with the large numbers of hunters now afield, survival means hiding.

In the 1960's, I used to take a trophy buck—often with an antler spread in excess of 30 inches—every year, most often by catching the buck browsing early or late or by spooking him out of the brush and onto the opposite open slope of a ravine. In those days, I wouldn't go into the timber; the hunting there was too hard and required too much concentration. It was many years before I could finally bring myself to hunt in the timber, and then I did it only after several years of shooting small bucks and not even seeing anything that could be considered a trophy animal.

The first time I hunted the timber, I was dragged into it. I had seen a big buck browsing at the edge of some timber late one evening. He was too far away to risk a shot in the poor light, and it would have been dark by the time I could make a stalk. But he was the biggest buck I had seen in years. In camp that night, I couldn't get the vision of that big, heavy rack out of my mind.

I returned to the stand of timber at first light, found the tracks, and began to follow. I was wearing blue jeans, and the snow and subfreezing temperatures had frozen them hard from the knees down. Occasionally, the frozen cuffs scraped together. At that point in my hunting career, I hadn't yet realized how keen a deer's senses are, and the thought of wearing quiet wool pants hadn't even crossed my mind. I followed the big tracks as they twisted and turned down through the spruces on the steep slope. Occasionally, I had to force my way through a thick growth of willows around a spring. Then I found his bed. Though it was below freezing and the snow that had thawed while he lay on it had frozen again, his droppings were still soft. I didn't think he had left the bed more than an hour before. The tracks led across the slope, through several shallow ravines where he had stopped to browse, and into some willows where he had battered one sapling almost barkless with his antlers. The brown strips of willow bark lay on the snow. Then he had gone on, meandering at times, moving straight and purposefully at others.

I followed the trail for several hours. It was cold in the timber; the rifle hung from the sling on my shoulder, and my hands were plunged deep into my coat pockets. I stepped across a small stream. The willows that bordered it scraped against my hard-frozen pants, and there in the gloom was the buck. He was lying down and staring at me. Then, he was up and gone in one motion. I didn't even have time to pull my hands out of my pockets.

That encounter still did not impress on me the importance of hunting the timber. I had spent too many years hunting the old way on open slopes where the bucks browsed placidly. To me, that timber buck was just a random occurrence.

The following year, I hunted the same country and concentrated on the rolling hills and shallow ravines on top of the big plateau. The land was open, and you could take your time, take a rest for your rifle, and pot the buck at your leisure. The mainstay was marksmanship. I saw a few bucks that season in the open country but nothing that could be considered a big buck. There were big tracks, though, and it was beginning to dawn on me that they had been made at night.

Where, I wondered, did the big deer spend their days? It could only be in the timber. That realization came suddenly and with force. The light bulb turned on. With some things, I'm a slow learner.

Full of enthusiasm, I moved into the timber, certain that I was making the right move. I walked down the same trail I had followed the preceding year when I had gone after that big buck. There were big tracks in the shadowy gloom. One set was on the trail I was following; others crossed it. I moved quietly on the needle-duff, remembering the year before, carrying the rifle almost as I would carry a shotgun when approaching a covey of quail. The buck was there in the deep shadows, wraith-like, his nose working to find out what had made him uneasy. At the shot, so out of place in the silent timber, the buck dropped without a quiver. I gloated, not at the buck, a very good four-point (Western count), but at the realization that I had finally found out where the big bucks were.

Stalking and tracking big bucks in the timber forced me to learn new skills. I had to become more of a hunter. No longer could I rely on my rifle's ability to hold a five-inch, 300-yard group. I had to move quietly and with the wind in my favor. I had to strain to see as far into the shadows as possible to detect the buck before he saw me. I had to be ready at all times with the rifle in my hands. I had to learn to pay more attention to sign. I learned to tell one set of tracks from another. I began to be able to tell how long ago the buck had browsed or urinated or scraped, and to tell whether the buck was traveling or looking for a place to bed. I had to move slowly, perhaps spending all day to get through a stand of timber and blowdowns less than a mile long. In the old days, I was known for covering large expanses of country. In the old days, that had paid off, but no longer.

Stillhunting or tracking in the timber makes a man a complete hunter. It's not enough to be good at tracking, or to hunt quietly, or to be a good shot, or to know the country and to see well. The best timber hunter does all of these well and all at the same time. Falling down in just one of these skills at any given moment can mean the escape of a trophy buck.

Another advantage of hunting the timber is that you can do it all day, even when the deer have bedded down. One afternoon, I was following a large set of tracks through a stand of spruce and fir. The area was full of deer tracks, and it was difficult not to lose the ones I was following in the maze. I was concentrating so hard on moving quietly and following the tracks that I nearly stepped on the buck, which apparently had been snoozing. He jumped up less than five yards away and crashed off through the blowdowns, frightening me out of my wits. Had I been more aware and looking ahead as I moved through the timber, I might have collected that buck.

Stillhunting can be just as effective in the timber as tracking. It is helpful, though, to know a particular stand of timber. Most stands include good areas for bedding, frequently used game trails, and places where the deer can grab an afternoon snack. If the stillhunter knows where these different areas are located, he stands a better chance of taking a buck.

One stand of spruce and fir that I am particularly familiar with is located in northern Utah. The surrounding country sustains heavy hunting pressure. I've been hunting it for years. In the timber, which is on a slope that faces north, is a steep ravine. One side of the ravine faces west, and the soil is so shallow that no large trees grow on it. Bitterbrush, some mountain mahogany, cliff rose, and forbs—all good deer browse—grow there. Above the ravine, there are large evergreens. The bucks, if undisturbed, lie underneath the trees. They are only a few yards from food or, in the other direction, thick, impenetrable blowdowns and timber. If I'm not following a set of tracks, I usually stillhunt toward that open slope. I've killed one good buck there and missed chances at several others.

Every hunter who has spent some time in the timber knows a lot about the wind. It's always good to keep it in your face, and it is always nice if the buck you are following is cooperative and moves into it. As often as not, however, it doesn't happen that way. A buck is as apt to move with the wind as into it, and he often beds in a place that is nearly impossible to approach without letting him scent you. In such situations, you have to anticipate what the buck will do. It helps to know the lay of the land, the game trails, deer habits in the area, and the normal wind direction at various times of the day. The wind normally blows uphill with the warming temperatures after sunup and becomes more dense and blows downhill with cooling temperatures.

Suddenly, mule-deer hunting has become complicated. Now, the hunter not only has to know the habits of the deer but the intricacies of the country as well. To me, that is the best of all possible hunting. You choose some timber where deer are abundant and hunt it year after year, learning all a hunter needs to know about it and disturbing it as little as possible so that the bucks don't move out.

Every hunter, though, has to hunt a stand of timber for the first time. Most hunters, due to lack of time or commitment, will never really learn a patch of timber. Even so, there is a way to go about it. If there are big deer tracks that aren't too old, and even though the buck is moving with the wind, there is still a decent chance of taking him.

Late one season, I was following a set of big tracks in snow that had fallen earlier that morning. The breeze was quartering in from behind me over my left shoulder. I had been hunting in timber for several years and knew that the buck, if he behaved anything like most of the other big bucks I'd hunted, would make a buttonhook, not unlike the one a football receiver makes as he runs his pass pattern. I guessed that the buck would do this below his trail to be downwind and to one side of it so that he could scent anything following him. The best chance I had was to make loops downwind of the trail, returning to the track every 100 yards or so—a pretty fair distance when you are stalking very slowly in timber—to be sure that I hadn't passed the buck in his bed. If I did it right, I figured I had a good chance to get a shot. It was nearly midday, and I was relatively sure that the buck had bedded down.

I was in my third loop downwind of the trail when I sensed that something was about to happen. I didn't discount that feeling or try to rationalize it away. I stopped, my thumb on the safety and the rifle held a little higher so I could bring it up more quickly, and looked carefully around for perhaps 20 minutes. Then, I took a step forward and saw some branches that looked suspiciously like antler tines. An ear twitched, and the "branches" moved. I eased the rifle up, forcing myself into that quiet, controlled state you shoot from if you do it right. I waited, hoping the buck would step clear of the blowdowns. He was uneasy. He probably had heard some faint noise I had made, or perhaps he was relying on some sixth sense of his own, but he hadn't located me. I was downwind, so he could not smell me. The buck, still uneasy, stepped silently forward, his nose working, his ears cocked, until his neck was clear.

That was a good buck, five points to the side (12 points Eastern count) and very fat. He was also quite old. His molars were worn nearly to the gum. He'd gotten old by staying in the timber, at least during hunting season.

Another method of hunting in timber is taking a stand along a well-used trail. I am not much of a stand hunter because it's sheer torture for me to be inactive for very long, so I seldom employ this method. One season, I was hunting with a lady friend. I knew where there was a heavily used trail through the timber, and I posted her behind a big fir tree above the trail. An hour or so after I'd left her, I'd heard a shot. When I returned, she was standing over a fat forkhorn. The buck had walked down the trail below her, and she had killed him cleanly. A moment after her shot, a good four-pointer had run up the trail and almost trampled her. Apparently, the second buck had been confused about the direction of the shot that had echoed through the timber.

Often, large stands of pine or spruce/fir have open areas within them that offer the resident deer excellent food without their ever having to leave the safety of the timber, even at night. These areas may be steep, shallow-soiled slopes exposed to the south or west that don't hold enough moisture for large trees, or they may be openings around water that have been kept clear of trees by beavers. Occasionally, they may be fairly large meadows. When you find a place like that and see a good set of tracks, you've got a real chance to take a good buck if you hunt carefully.

I know of several such places, one of them in Montana. It is near the northern boundary of Yellowstone National Park. It is on a low mountain covered on its northern and eastern slopes mainly by fir and spruce, and on its drier and warmer southern and western slopes with lodgepole pine. On top of the mountain is a sagebrush opening that drops into an open ravine, which is dry except in the spring. The ravine is thick with good deer browse, and it slopes gently to the east before being swallowed up by the timber. The whole area is perhaps 300 yards long and maybe 200 wide. It is an excellent place to find big bucks. I've photographed deer there a number of times, but I haven't hunted there yet. Indeed, I wouldn't want to disturb the place and chase the bucks out; they might never return. I don't think I could kill a buck there without a twinge of conscience.

Hunting the timber has given me a new enthusiasm for hunting big mule deer bucks. It is a little like an old man suddenly finding his wife attractive again. After years of watching trophy hunting deteriorate, of seeing or hearing about fewer and fewer big bucks, all of a sudden I've found a way to get at big heads again.

This very good buck with a 34-inch spread was taken in the trees.

8

Watch A Trail To Take A Trophy

The sun had just set, and I was sitting in the same spot I had occupied on the previous five evenings—the lip of a tiny ravine down which ran a faint deer trail. Before long, it would again be too dark to shoot, and I would again climb over the lip of the ravine and walk back along the top of the plateau to camp.

Each day I had checked the large, fresh deer tracks along the trail. A good buck was using it regularly, but he was using it at night. The tracks led from a big stand of spruce and fir through the little ravine to a hillside of bitterbrush, cliff rose and mountain mahogany. In the morning, before it began to get light, the buck would return to the timber, where he apparently spent the daylight hours. I hadn't seen him, but I knew he was there. His presence permeated the ravine. I even had visions of what his rack must look like.

It was nearly dark, almost too dark to shoot, when I sensed something at the edge of the trees. Perhaps I'd seen, just on the edge of true perception, some little flicker of movement in the shadows of trees. Or perhaps it was just the sixth sense. I stared at the place where the faint trail was swallowed up by the trees. There it was again! But what was it?

A big buck stepped out of the timber, stared down the trail for a moment and then walked toward me. The buck must have been hungry because he was leaving the cover to feed earlier than usual. It was just what I'd been hoping for.

I let the crosshairs—almost too faint to see in the gathering darkness—center on the point of his shoulder as he quartered toward me, and then I squeezed the trigger. For a moment, I lost the buck and the ravine to the muzzle flash of the .270. My vision readjusted, but I couldn't see the deer. I hadn't heard him run out of the ravine. I walked down to the trail.

The buck lay on the trail, and his antlers lived up to my fantasies. I hurriedly dressed him in what was, by then, darkness. As I again hiked across the plateau to camp, I could not remember seeing a more spectacular, star-filled sky.

Feeding And Bedding Trails

With the number of hunters afield these days, most big bucks have become more or less nocturnal. They have to do so to survive to trophy proportions. Nevertheless, there is always a chance to catch them as they leave cover on the way to feed just as it gets dark, or just as they return to it with the first faint light of dawn. It may be that the hunter has to wait four or five days, but if he is sure that a big buck is using the trail, he may eventually catch him. Of course, if the hunter only wants meat, younger, more naive bucks are common along feeding and bedding trails during daylight hours.

Before taking a stand on a feeding and bedding trail, it is often necessary to locate a buck without ever actually laying eyes on him. Pre-season scouting is a must. If you find large tracks, and they appear regularly on a trail, it's a good trail to watch.

Once I've found a likely trail, I get to my stand long before it gets light and stay until after sunup. I have previously determined what the wind does at that time of the day in that place and have positioned myself so that the deer won't catch my scent. As a rule, I don't sit and wait all day. During midday, I may stillhunt through a patch of timber, or hunt some adjacent country, or perhaps return to camp for lunch and a nap.

I return to the trail sometime during midafternoon. It is often necessary to sit in a different place in the evening. As often as not, the wind is blowing from a different direction because the air is warm and less dense and therefore rising in the afternoon, as opposed to cold, dense and flowing downhill before sunup. Once you've found a good spot to sit, one that gives you a good view of the trail, settle into some sagebrush or other shrubs. Show only a low profile, make no sudden movements and be as inconspicuous as possible. Mule deer have better vision than they are given credit for, and they are especially sensitive to movement. Mule deer also have the best hearing of any big-game animal on the continent, so don't make unusual sounds.

Bucks may not leave and return to cover by the same trail. Last fall, I spent about 10 days trying to photograph a group of big bucks in southwestern Montana. Three of the bucks stayed together much of the time. They would feed out of the timber in the evening along one trail and return in the morning on another trail several hundred yards away. Those bucks probably became more nocturnal, and their routine more flexible, with the approach of hunting season.

Escape And Cover Trails

Escape trails or trails between two types of cover can also be productive under the right circumstances. Escape trails frequently lead to a stand of heavy timber or brush, an inaccessible canyon or some other place where a wise old mule-deer buck can lose himself. Sometimes, deer escape through natural crossing places such as saddles or the heads of canyons.

A smart trophy buck may not necessarily take the shortest or easiest route to safety when disturbed. In most of the West, mule deer are heavily hunted. A big buck doesn't get big by being a dummy. He has been around and knows what a hunter is likely to do. If he is being driven through a patch of timber, he often knows that hunters are probably waiting for him on the other side. As a consequence, he may do what the hunter least expects, or go another way to some distant refuge.

When I used to hunt mule deer regularly in northern Utah, I would often go to a particular saddle on opening morning. As regular as taxes, and as unwelcome to the deer, one group of hunters would make a big drive through the timber at the head of a canyon to force deer out over the saddle above the place where the hunters had posted their standers. Most of the men were meat hunters and were happy to get any buck that was foolish enough to show himself. The hunters had been in the country for years and knew that the saddle was a natural crossing as well as an escape hatch.

The drive typically began with more than a dozen riders at the lower end of the big stand of timber in the canyon bottom. At some prearranged time, after the hunters above had posted themselves along the escape trail, the riders moved through the timber in a great crescent, the points forward along the edge of the timber. Undoubtedly, some deer slipped through the line of riders, but many more headed up through the timber and through the saddle to where the standers were waiting. There was always a great deal of shooting.

I knew the country better than the drivers did, and unknown to them, I also participated. There was a small but deep ravine that came into the timber at right angles to the escape trail through the saddle. The ravine trail was invisible unless you were right on top of it. The slopes above it were covered with aspen, chokecherry and a few firs. For several years, I'd get to the ravine before the riders started their drive. I shot some fairly decent bucks along that ravine, larger than any deer that the hunters in the saddle ever took. Once, I missed a chance at a real mossyhorn. The buck was trotting up the ravine bottom but stopped suddenly, sensing something amiss. I could see his big rack, but the rest of him was screened by the brush. He paused a few moments, but then turned and ran straight up the hill through the aspens. I couldn't get a shot. The hunters in the saddle above didn't get many big bucks because only the younger bucks were foolish enough to go through the saddle. The older bucks either wouldn't be in the stand of timber to begin with or would run up the ravine I'd found. They probably had other escape routes as well.

Crossing Trails

Crossing trails are very good places to ambush a buck. Typical natural crossings include trails through a saddle to another canyon, or a trail that leads out of the head of a canyon. Trails through timber or brush along a bench are also good bets.

These crossing trails may also be used as escape trails when a buck is hard-pressed, or as a trail from one feeding area to another or from a bedding area to a feeding area. More often than not, however, they are just ways for a buck to get from one canyon to the next.

Early in my hunting career, I'd sit at a particular saddle in a range of fairly high mountains. I'd heard that saddles were good places to ambush a buck. I sat in the saddle for several evenings, waiting along a trail that passed through it to another canyon. By that time, I was ready to settle for any buck that showed itself. It was evening, I was cold and hungry, and I was getting ready to head for camp. Then, a deer suddenly materialized in the saddle, and then another and another. One was a small three-point buck (six-point Eastern count). Suddenly, I had an attack of acute buck fever. I found the buck in the scope, pushed the safety off and yanked a shot. Of course, I missed. I fired again as the deer trotted through the saddle, and then again. Then, the deer were gone. I'd blown it, I was sure, but I'd read somewhere that a hunter should always check for blood after firing at an animal, so I walked over and looked. There were splatters of blood in the dust of the trail just where it started to drop down the slope. The light was about gone when I stumbled over the buck lying in the trail.

Migration Trails

Migration trails lead down from the high country to the lower winter range. They can offer some of the best trophy hunting imaginable. If a hunter catches the migration correctly, he'll have a chance to look over a number of good bucks and take his pick. At least it happened that way on the two occasions when I was lucky enough to catch a muley migration. I've talked with other hunters who have had similar experiences.

Unfortunately, for migration-trail hunting to be effective, you need heavy snow or at least a strong approaching storm front in the high country. Deer and other animals can sense the dropping barometric pressure of the approaching storm and head for lower country. To increase your chances of catching a large downward mule deer migration, try to get deer permits in areas that have late hunts. Several Western states offer permits for hunts that take place in November and December. Then, it helps a great deal to talk to the local ranchers and hunters; they often know the best places to go. In lieu of that, or perhaps in addition, study topographic maps. Mule deer like to migrate along ridges that overlook a steep canyon, though they sometimes go down a broad, more-open canyon. If the migration is already in progress, it is a simple matter to check for tracks and heavily used trails.

Late one very cold December, I was hunting just east of Big Piney, Wyoming. I'd been hunting the plateaus and large, deep ravines that cut through the foothill country of the high mountains just to the west. I had jumped some deer, mostly does and small bucks from the ravines, but I'd seen nothing worth shooting. By afternoon, it had clouded up and begun to get warm—a sign that a storm was approaching. By evening, deer were moving down the draws and ridges to lower country, but I didn't see a good buck.

The storm hit that night and dropped 15 inches of snow in Big Piney and 20 in the foothills. Undoubtedly, there was more in the mountains. Deer were everywhere, and most were moving downward. The country had filled almost overnight with the deer that had been in the high mountains, and they were still coming down. They followed well-used trails along the ridges, where the wind blew away some of the snow. I saw somewhere in the neighborhood of 200 deer that morning, and some were good bucks following distant ridges. I made several stalks but never got a shot. By afternoon, I realized that my best chance would be to sit along one of the trails and wait.

I found a wind-twisted pine overlooking a well-used trail and built a fire. The cold, dense wind was blowing down the ridge, and it carried the smoke and my scent away from the deer. Every 20 minutes or so, a band of deer walked down the trail not 40 yards away. Once, a medium-size four-pointer came by, but I let him pass. By evening, I'd seen perhaps 100 deer on that trail.

The fire had burned down to ashes, and I was stamping my feet to restore circulation before leaving for the road when a good buck came over the ridge and down the trail. He wasn't quite as big as some of those I'd seen on distant ridges earlier, but I put the crosshairs on his shoulder and squeezed the trigger. He pitched forward at the shot and lay still.

Since that time more than 25 years ago, I have only been fortunate enough to catch one other muley migration, and I had similar results. I often dream of doing it again.

Bedding And Feeding Areas

Trails aren't the only place to ambush a buck. Bedding and feeding areas are just as good, if you know how. I've read and have had hunters tell me that they found a buck's bed, waited for him to return and then shot him. I'm pretty skeptical. Though a buck will usually bed more than once in the same general area, I think it is only coincidence, except in rare instances, that he will lay up again in the same exact place. Just the same, if you can find where a buck regularly spends the daylight hours, and it will usually be in thick timber or brush, you stand a fair chance of collecting him. I know of one place in the Wasatch Mountains where one or more bucks usually bed. It is on an open, west-facing slope in the center of a big stand of timber. They usually bed near the top of the slope, where they are only a hop away from thick, impenetrable timber and brush if danger should threaten. Merely by standing up, they can take a midday snack of cliff rose, bitterbrush or mountain mahogany on the slope. If I'm of a mind to hunt the place, I usually sit in the timber on the opposite slope and wait.

Feeding areas can be just as good, I suppose, but I haven't had such good luck with them. Favorite deer browse in most of the West includes bitterbrush, mountain and curl-leaf mahogany, cliff rose, sagebrush and a variety of forbs. It's not really necessary to identify these plants, though it may help. If a hunter can find deer tracks meandering in a certain location, the deer are probably feeding there. He simply finds a place in the cover downwind of the spot and waits. He increases his odds by getting there before first light and staying until darkness.

Whether waiting along a feeding/bedding escape, crossing or migration trail, or at a bedding or feeding site, there are some basics to keep in mind. First, be sure that deer are using the trail or the bedding or feeding area.

Learn to recognize big tracks, then make sure that there are some reasonably fresh ones around. While scouting an area, study wind direction at various times of the day, and when it comes down to the hunting, position yourself downwind accordingly. Don't scout an area too much and frighten the deer out. It doesn't take much disturbance to chase a wise old mule deer buck into the next canyon. Similarly, disturb the place as little as possible when hunting. Be as inconspicuous as possible. Make no unnecessary movements, break up your outline with brush, and be quiet! Again, mule deer have better vision than they are given credit for, especially when it comes to movement, and they have the best hearing of any game animal on the continent. They also have an excellent sense of smell.

The nice thing about ambushing bucks is that it is a pleasant way to spend time. Other wildlife, as well as deer, may amble along. I've seen bobcats, bears, moose, elk and bighorn sheep shuffling along "deer trails." Once, I even saw a mountain lion. And ambushing a buck doesn't take the body and endurance of a decathlete, either. Heavyweight old men stand as good a chance to ambush a buck as the young and lean.

An adult buck using a feeding and bedding trail.

9

On The Right Track
For Muleys

Tracking trophy mule deer involves more than getting on a track and following to its end. Often, it requires moving away from the track and returning only periodically to confirm that you're still on the trail. And it always involves interpreting what the buck has done (and indirectly, its state of mind at the time) and, most importantly, predicting what it's likely to do. But first, a hunter has to learn to identify tracks and strides made by a trophy buck.

Strides And Tracks

Mule deer seldom run without cause. This is even more true of fat and wise trophy bucks. Unless especially frightened, a buck will walk or trot from one place to another. Moving slowly saves energy and allows the buck to be more alert.

Walking

When a deer walks, the hind feet are placed almost exactly in the print left by the forehoof. The walking stride of a big buck is between 23 and 26 inches long. If the trail seems to meander around shrubs and forbs, the buck was feeding on those plants. If the track is wandering with little or no evidence of feeding, the buck is looking for a place to bed down. If you're on the track of a good buck, and it starts to meander without evidence of feeding, in all probability the animal is very near and watching its backtrail, so be alert. If a walking track is laid out in a straight line with little or no wandering, the buck is traveling. In such a case, you can follow the tracks quickly and with less regard for noise and wind.

Trotting

The trotting stride is used almost as often as walking. Last fall, while I was driving through Wyoming, a large buck crossed the road in front of me and trotted across an alfalfa field. I stopped the pickup, grabbed a tape measure and measured the strides where the buck crossed the field. The strides were 35 to 38 inches between prints, fairly typical for an adult buck. When a mature buck trots, the hoofprints will appear individually, and the stride will measure from 33 to 40 inches, depending on the rate of trot and the size of the buck.

Galloping

When a buck gallops, it's frightened. The right forehoof strikes the ground first, and the left front foot hits a short distance in front of the print left by the right forehoof. As the hind legs come forward, the right hind foot contacts the ground first, followed by the left. When you're looking at a galloping track, the prints of the forefeet are behind the prints of the hind feet, and the left tracks are a bit ahead of the right. The gallop is an energy-consuming

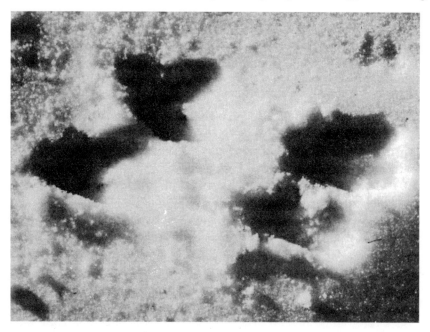

Tracks of a bounding buck; rear tracks print ahead of front tracks.

MULE DEER TRACKS AND STRIDES

large buck
in soft
soil or
snow

Smaller
buck

Very large buck-3¼"-4"

Left hind   Right hind

Left front   Right front

<u>Bounding</u> <u>mule deer</u>

stride, and as a rule, a buck won't use it for long. Usually, it will revert back to a trot as soon as it's prudent, and stop to rest and see if anything is following. Almost invariably, when a buck stops to watch its backtrail, it will do so from a stand of timber or brush.

Bounding

When a trophy buck bounds, it must have been unusually frightened. Bounding consumes more energy than any other stride, and a buck will do it for only a short time.

The strides of nine adult bucks I measured ranged from 22 feet to 29 feet on level ground. Naturally, the stride's length would depend on how badly a buck is frightened, his size and terrain. Bounding may appear awkward, but it's effective to get a buck over rough, uneven terrain in a big hurry.

When I first started hunting mule deer back in the 1960's, now and then I'd run into a hunter who understood the rudiments of tracking. These days, however, few people practice this art. Usually, the first problem novice trackers face is identifying a mature mule buck's track. The hoof itself is wider than those of small bucks and does, it is longer, and it is rounder at the tip. In very rocky country, such as in the rimrocks of western Colorado, southern Arizona and many other places, an old buck's track may appear so rounded at the tip that it looks like a small version of a Hereford steer's track.

The front track of a particularly large buck I took in 1986 measured 4¼ inches in length (excluding dewclaws) and three inches in width. A more typical track for an adult buck is 3½ to four inches in length. The stride of big bucks is naturally longer, and they drag their feet a bit in soft soil or shallow snow. An adult buck's toes usually point outward somewhat, though the degree may be subtle.

Techniques And Tactics

Determining A Track's Age

Determining the age of tracks can be tricky business. The only way to get good at it is to get experience. The best way to practice is to make tracks of your own in various soil types and under conditions common in the areas where you'll be hunting. Note how they change in two hours, in five, in 10, in 24. When I first started to learn, I carried a belt knife with a handle made from a deer's foot. For years, I'd press the hoof into various soil types around camp and note the change over time. Along with field experience, that little exercise taught me more about aging tracks than everything I've read on tracking combined. Humidity, temperature, soil types, weather and other factors must be considered when aging tracks, and only practice can teach you to age them correctly.

Watching The Backtrail

A big muley buck will typically pause just inside timber or brush to watch its backtrail. Back when I was learning the game, I read countless stories about deer pausing in an opening to stare back at the hunters, usually broadside. I believed them. Because it seldom happened to me, I assumed that I was unlucky.

Then one day, I flushed a buck from some timber, and because it didn't pause to look back, I took up its trail. At first, it bounded through some dead-falls, then it slowed to a gallop and finally slowed to a less tiring trot. Whenever the buck came to a large clearing, it would circle and pause on the other side to see whether I was still on its trail. Eventually, I got wise and circled far downwind of a small opening. I caught the buck standing in the shadows of the timber, watching. I got a shot as it bounded away, but only managed to topple a spruce sapling. However, I've used the tactic since and it works.

The Buttonhook Maneuver

An old buck will normally make a buttonhook—similar to one a football receiver makes when running a pass pattern—on the downwind side of the backtrail before it beds. That way it can smell or often see any danger following. Remember, bucks meander, usually without feeding, just before they bed down. So if you're on the track of a buck looking for a bed, start making loops on the downwind side of the trail in the general direction the buck is moving. The buck may look for a bed for some time, or it may find one that suits it almost immediately. Usually, when it begins to meander it won't be far off, so be very careful. Return to the buck's trail occasionally for confirmation. If you pass the end of the trail, make loops back toward the area where you last saw the track. In all likelihood, the buck will be bedded somewhere along the way, so be ready and carry your gun as you would if you were approaching a setter on point. I've taken at least a dozen good bucks this way, and the technique has been proven for millennia by primitive hunters.

The first buck I tracked using the "loop technique" had been spooked by hunters far down a creek. I'd watched the buck from across a canyon as it made its way up a slope through thickets of oak scrub and chokecherry, then into a big stand of fir and spruce. By the time it entered the timber, it was moving at a slow trot. I didn't think that the buck would leave the timber because it didn't seem to be badly frightened when it entered. But it was alert and would be watching the backtrail carefully. I'd have to move slowly and quietly and be ready when the buck jumped. I knew that the deer would see me as soon as I'd see it, if not before.

One thing in my favor was a light, fresh snow, so the tracks were easy to see. I found where the buck entered the timber and moved slowly into the gloom of the trees. The day was warming, so the air was drifting uphill.

"He'll be above the trail," I told myself, and climbed uphill at a right angle to the trail. Although I kept my distance, I then moved parallel to the trail before returning to it a few hundred yards farther on. I could tell that the buck wasn't quite ready to bed down because the trail was laid out straight and purposefully. Two hundred yards farther into the timber, the trail angled uphill, across a slope and then made an aimless half-circle. The tracks revealed that several times, the buck had stopped to watch the backtrail. I was looping downwind and uphill of the trail when I caught a faint, yet unmistakable whiff of a heavy, musky odor. I strained to see into the shadows. Then there was crashing as the buck bounded off downhill. I took a shot, and luck was with me. The bullet caught the buck in the back of the neck.

Snow, of course, makes tracking easier. And tracking can be best after the first snow because even trophy bucks still believe that they blend in with the vegetation. I once tracked down a good buck that I had been hunting for a solid week. The animal was standing across a ravine in thick oak brush, but its dark body was perfectly obvious against the new snow. If there had been no snow on the ground, as was the situation the day before, the buck would have been all but invisible. I picked a path for the bullet through the brush and touched off the .270. The buck bounded hard for a few yards before collapsing.

Unique Track Characteristics

No tracks are identical. When you're after a particular buck, look for unique characteristics in the track—such as a chip or gouge in a hoof or some irregularity in stride—that you can use for identification. Then, all you have to do is look for that track to find out what the big buck has been doing or where it is going.

During one hot and dry season, I found the track of a very big buck. The tip of its right forehoof had been broken off. I followed the track through some red clay, and it was obvious that the buck left the track while the ground had been wet just after the last rainstorm, several weeks prior. The only fresh tracks I came across left by the buck were in the dust among a stand of fir trees. There were no fresh tracks on the hard ground outside the timber.

Then, as often happens with persistence, luck changed. One evening, the skies to the northwest clouded over, and lightning flickered across the parched land. It started raining shortly after dark and kept pouring much of the night. Despite puddles in my tent and water dripping into my ear, I was ecstatic. Any tracks I'd find in the morning would be fresh.

About midmorning, I found the chipped-hoof track where the buck had moved out of a tangle of aspen saplings. The trail wandered through an opening where the buck had browsed on rose hips and dried forbs. Then the trail crossed an open slope in a more or less straight line. I followed the trail quickly, knowing that the buck had a destination in mind.

A half-mile up a canyon, I lost the trail in a maze of other tracks. From the sign, apparently a half-dozen smaller deer had come down the canyon after the buck had passed, completely obliterating its track. As is necessary when tracking, I tried to analyze what the buck was intending do. I reasoned that because the buck had been traveling purposefully up the canyon, it would continue in the same direction for a while. All I had to do was move up the canyon beyond the maze of tracks to pick up the chipped-hoof print again. It worked, although it probably wouldn't have if I hadn't earlier noticed the distinguishing chip in the hoof. It wasn't long before the tracks began to meander, which told me that the buck was looking for a bed. I moved downwind off the trail about 50 yards, then eased along parallel to it. I knew that the buck would buttonhook downwind of its trail so that it could sense anything following. Indeed, it had. I jumped the buck at 15 yards in a tangle of fallen timber and got a quick, broadside shot that took it through the lungs. It was a large four-point (10-point Eastern count).

I got the buck as I do almost any good buck I get by tracking because I have learned to recognize what an old buck's track and stride looks like; I have learned to identify individual tracks; to interpret a buck's state of mind by the trail; and probably most importantly, to predict a buck's behavior by the trail it leaves. I got that buck because when it began to meander, I knew that it was looking for a bed, and when a trophy buck beds down, nine times out of 10 it'll do it downwind of its backtrail. I didn't get the buck because I found a trail and stubbornly followed it. If I'd done that, I would have come up empty-handed.

Although I know several whitetail hunters who are accomplished trackers, I haven't met a true mule deer tracker in at least a dozen years. If you do learn to track muleys, while most hunters are in camp during midday waiting for the deer to move in evening, you'll be out tracking a buck to its bed.

10

Those Huge Mule Deer

When I was 14, I killed my first big muley buck with a battered .303 rifle. It was a 268-pound four-pointer. That was thirty years ago, and since that time I've killed sixty more trophy bucks, in six Western states and in several Canadian Provinces. In that time, I've learned a lot about mule deer behavior.

One of the most important precepts in deer hunting, or any hunting, for that matter, is to hunt where there is plenty of "edge." It can be a spot where a dense coniferous forest and grasslands meet, or where islands of oak and sagebrush grass come together. These edges are by far the most productive areas for deer, elk, or a host of other game.

Primary Deer Feed

Deer, like most of our popular big game, is a species which prefers midsuccession plants. They thrive in areas where plant succession is in developmental stages. Plant succession in most areas of the West generally goes from grasses to forbs to shrubs and tall herbs and climaxes with trees. These midsuccessional plant species, shrubs, browse, and tall herbs, are primary deer feed. Edges are in midsuccession between one plant community and another. They often contain the bitterbrush, mountain mahogany, and other browse deer prefer. Also of primary importance to big game is that edge is usually only a few feet from cover and safety.

Another important principle in hunting trophy muleys is to work areas that receive relatively light pressure. These areas may or may not be remote. If they contain plenty of edge, it's a good bet that there are trophy bucks around. Areas may receive little hunting pressure because of remoteness, topography, denseness of vegetation, or simply because they don't look like deer country. No trophy buck would lie up within a quarter of a mile from a well-used 4WD-vehicle trail, or would he?

Hunt On The Edge

In dense stands of conifers, common in many parts of the Northwest and British Columbia, good areas to hunt are old "burns" or logging clearcuts. While I was doing summer work for the Forest Service in Idaho, 99 percent of the deer and elk I saw were in such areas. The increase of deer and elk in Idaho in recent years is attributed to the large number of forest fires and their consequent increasing of edge.

Check Old Burns

On a recent British Columbia moose hunt we would regularly check old burns, and virtually all of the deer seen were in such areas. Any clearing in dense timber is likely to be a concentration spot for deer. On a hunt in British Columbia our camp was set up on the edge of a small marsh, with abundant willow and other browse. One morning after a fresh snow, I stepped out of the tent into the midst of half-a-dozen mule deer. I grabbed a rifle, fumbled a cartridge into the chamber, and squeezed off a shot at a rapidly disappearing buck. The four-point piled up with a lung shot and we had our camp meat. In the surrounding dense spruce and fir we saw virtually no deer sign. (An exception to this would be prior to or during a storm.)

Other good places to hunt when in dense timber country are large blowdowns, common in many parts of the West, particularly in stands of lodgepole pine. Avalanches and tree diseases or parasites often create large clearings and increase edge.

Beaver Clearings

One of the most valuable creators of edge in the West is the beaver. He cuts down large amounts of aspen, cottonwood, and other trees, creating clearings and large areas of marginal land. One of my favorite hunting areas is just such a place. It is located in northern Utah, 30 miles east of Ogden. There are several large beaver dams with perhaps eight acres of downed aspen, at the head of a small canyon. The cutover areas are rampant with chokecherry, buckbrush, willows, aspen saplings, and other browse. Deer, elk, and moose congregate here. Grouse, bobcat, and rabbit are also common. This canyon, usually over-looked by most hunters, is a consistent producer of good deer. I have killed several here and have brought in friends who have taken good bucks. The best method for hunting this area is to take a stand in the afternoon and wait until deer feed out of the aspen into the clearings around dusk. Stillhunting, as it starts to get light, is also good.

Another, similar, area has also gotten me a good buck. There are several small beaver dams at the bottom of a canyon perhaps a quarter of a mile from a well-used jeep road. Due to the proximity of the road I had figured no buck of any size would frequent such a place, and consequently had never hunted this canyon. Apparently, other hunters were thinking the same thing.

Late one afternoon, more as a last resort than anything else, I decided to try the canyon. I started down the steep sides but decided to roll a boulder instead. As the boulder neared bottom a forkhorn bounded across the stream and started up the other side. Another two-point followed. An instant later a huge buck bounded across the stream and started up through the aspen. I was astounded. What was a wise old mossyhorn doing so close to a road? About halfway up the opposite slope he paused in a small clearing. I aimed above the back line with my .270 and squeezed. The rifle roared, the buck made a frantic leap, ran in a small circle, and dropped. The 130-grain bullet had taken him through the heart at nearly 400 yards. There was no hunter sign in the canyon bottom at all. This canyon, too obvious to receive much hunting pressure and with plenty of edge, was an almost perfect hideout for the buck.

There are numerous areas throughout the West with large amounts of edge not created by fire, beaver, logging, or man. These areas can be large, grassy parks breaking up stands of pine, islands of aspen or oak in a sea of sagebrush, or grassland-chaparral communities. One such area, west of Big Piney, Wyoming, consistently produces good deer. This country is predominantly sagebrush plateau with aspen on the north-facing slopes of the shallow canyons. The edges between the aspen and sagebrush communities produce a variety of browse palatable to deer. Ninety-eight percent of the deer are found here. Probably 100 percent feed here. The few bucks that manage to survive to trophy size are here only at night, when they feed. During the day they hole up in gullies, ravines, and other less-obvious places. This country, subject to comparatively heavy hunting pressure, has very little aspen compared to the total land area. These aspen pockets, the obvious place to hunt, receive intense hunting pressure throughout the long season. In order to survive to trophy size, bucks have to hide elsewhere. Those that don't wind up in the deep freeze.

Edge in most of the Ruby Range of the Humboldt National Forest of northeast Nevada is restricted. A large percentage of these lands below 7,500 feet are sagebrush-grass country. Up to 8,500 feet the cover is still relatively scarce or limited in locality. Stands of aspen, juniper, and a few other small trees and large shrubs break up the sagebrush-grassland expanses. Here is where most of the deer congregate. These edges provide feed, and cover is only a few jumps away. Springs and small creeks are common. These areas also receive the heaviest hunting pressure, and by far the heaviest deer harvest are from such locations. Deer, in order to die of old age, must find less obvious places to hide.

After three days of preseason scouting I had seen scores of does, fawns, and forkhorns, but no big bucks. Most of my scouting was in areas with heavy brush, the obvious place to look, and that was where most of the deer were sighted. The afternoon before opening day, I had spotted a small, dense, isolated pocket of aspen and shrubs high on a steep, relatively bare, slope. I decided to hunt toward it in the morning. It was nearly 10 o'clock by the time I had hunted my way up to the pocket of brush. It was perhaps 30 feet wide and 60 feet long in a more or less oblong shape. It didn't look like much. I tossed a few stones into the tangle. Nothing happened. I walked closer. I was about 10 yards from the brush when an immense buck crashed out. I had to sprint up the hill to get a shot over the aspen. The buck was quartering away at 50 yards. I yanked off a shot and missed clean. I settled down and took him as he was disappearing over the ridge. He was a very good four-point. Since that pocket of brush was so small, virtually all of it was in some stage of developmental succession. Most of it was usable deer feed. The aspen at the center were scarcely 10 feet high, and saplings, chokecherry, and brush got progressively smaller the nearer they came to the edge between the start of the grass-sage. This pocket of brush satisfied the buck's need for food as well as shelter, and he received little disturbance from man here.

Bucks—Where You Least Expect Them

Though deer populations are always most dense in areas with abundant edge, the really cagey old bucks are often where you least expect them. Deer season in northern Utah is commonly coincidental to the downward migration of domestic sheep herds. During the 1967 deer season, I would daily climb to the rim of a particular basin and wait until dark. I'd see does, fawns, small bucks, and an occasional mature buck nearly every day. I figured it was only a matter of time before I'd get a chance at a real trophy. The fifth day of the season I hiked to the edge of the basin and looked in. It was filled with noisy, smelly sheep. I pondered my next move.

At that moment a huge buck jumped out of a tangle of aspen and oak and raced up the opposite slope. He had been lying up within 15 feet of several sheep. I fired as he bounced up the hill. He increased his pace. I fired again. The buck sat down, pitched over backward, and lay still. The first shot had creased the neck and the second had entered between the shoulder blades and exited through the brisket. He had a massive, though uneven, five-point rack and later weighed in at 220 pounds. Was he intentionally traveling with the sheep, knowing he would get little hunting pressure with them? Or had he moved into the basin the night before? I'll never know for sure, but I like to think he had adopted the sheep as traveling companions.

Hunt Where Hunters Don't Go

Canyons that receive little hunting pressure because of the steepness of terrain are often trophy-buck hotspots. One such canyon, draining into the South Fork of the Ogden River east of Ogden, Utah, has produced my best buck to date. Though a jeep road runs past the canyon head and along its north ridge, few hunters attempt to work it. The slopes are steep. Fingers of sage break up the dense stands of aspen at the canyon head. Oak scrub, sagebrush, and aspen cover the canyon sides. Spruce and fir, intermixed with aspen, dot the canyon bottom. Dense tangles of aspen, chokecherry, and willow, broken by limestone outcrops, climb the steep north wall. Edge is abundant. Cover and feed are always nearby.

The deer population is high. It is no trick to see forty deer a day in the canyon, and mature bucks are common. During the 1965 deer season I would hurry home from school (I was then a freshman at Weber State College in Ogden), jump in the 4WD vehicle, and drive up to the canyon daily. I usually didn't arrive until about 5 P.M. I'd then either take a stand or stillhunt along the canyon sides.

One day I parked the vehicle at the end of the road and started hunting toward the canyon bottom. When I got to the bottom I started working up the sides toward the canyon head. I spotted deer constantly; the biggest problem was to avoid spooking them. About halfway up the canyon I walked into a group of elk which crashed through the aspen toward the canyon head. They probably would've spooked anything above so I turned around and headed back. I caught a movement about 200 yards below where the jeep was parked. I screwed the variable-power scope to 9X and looked. Even at 800 yards the buck looked big. His spread extended well beyond the ear tips.

He was feeding along the edge of a dense tangle of aspen perhaps 5 yards out into the open. One jump and he would be in heavy brush. I started the stalk. Slow, deliberate movement—if the buck couldn't get my scent or outline—shouldn't spook him, since deer were feeding throughout the canyon. After a stalk of about 400 yards I came to an aspen with a fork about 4 feet from the ground. I took off my jacket, laid it in the crotch, and lay the rifle across it. The buck was staring intently in my direction. I put the crosshairs about a foot above his back and squeezed. The 7mm magnum bellowed and kicked up dust above his back. I had over estimated bullet drop. I lowered the crosshairs and squeezed again. The rifle recoiled, the buck hunched, wobbled a few steps, and dropped. His spread was 32 inches with no abnormal points.

The mountainous country just northeast of Cokeville, Wyoming, has one of the highest deer population densities of any place I have hunted. If I see less than forty deer in a day's hunting, I consider it poor. I have seen as many as seventy-eight deer in a day. This country has plenty of cover. Thick stands of lodgepole pine, aspen, and fir are broken by sagebrush, juniper, and grass. Edge is extremely plentiful. Open grassy parks are common, and deer are nearly everywhere.

This easily accessible country receives fairly heavy hunting pressure from small armies of nonresidents as well as the locals. Few bucks reach trophy proportions, and those that do seek out remote canyons and crags. A good bet, when hunting this country, is to look for areas that, for some reason or other, receive little hunting pressure. There are many small, steep canyons running off the main ridges. These usually don't look like they would be worth the effort to hunt. They are small, steep, rocky, and often contain dense stands of conifers, aspen, or other brush. Few hunters want to expend the effort to claw through them. These canyons are where the big bucks hang out. I spent a week working this country, concentrating on the larger valleys and canyons. I saw in the neighborhood of 300 deer during the week. All but six were either forkhorns, does, or fawns. Six were bucks in the 3½ to 4½-year-old class. Some were fair, but none were trophies by any stretch of the imagination.

On the next to my last day of hunting I had worked up onto the ridge of a very steep, small canyon. The canyon, scarcely 400 yards wide from ridge to ridge, contained dense stands of aspen and other shrubs. I tossed a few stones into the tangle. Nothing happened. I started working my way down through the brush. About halfway down I jumped some deer. They crashed through the undergrowth below me and started up the opposite slope. I caught a glimpse of them just as they were going over the ridge. They were both immense bucks, far better than any I had seen in the previous six days. Mule deer characteristically pause to look back at whatever spooked them before they top out, but these bucks were in high gear until they were out of sight.

The next morning I worked into a nearly identical canyon. Its head originated on a ridge that had, during the course of the season, received heavy hunting pressure. A road passed by less than 200 yards from the start of the canyon, which dropped off sharply to a valley 1,000 feet below. Dense stands of conifers occupied the north-facing slope. Aspen ran up the canyon bottom to a heavy growth at the head. Scattered juniper and sage, broken by slides of jagged rock, covered the south-facing slope. I worked down into the spruce and fir.

Near the bottom I jumped what appeared to be a good buck in heavy jackpine. The buck hit the bottom and started up the other side. I sprinted toward a small clearing 25 yards to my right. The buck had slowed to a walk as he made his way up a large rockslide. I sat down and put the scope on the buck. Though he wasn't as good as the two I had jumped the day before, I decided to take him. I put the crosshairs between the shoulder blades and squeezed. The buck dropped as if pole-axed, slid a few feet, and lay still. The 130-grain .270 bullet entered just behind the shoulder blades, broke the spine, and exited through the brisket. Though the buck had only three points per side (excluding brow tines), the tines were very long and their spread was 29 inches.

If you want to consistently take trophy muleys, it's a good idea to learn to think like one. Learn to recognize mid-successional plant types; it's not hard. They're shrubs, tall herbs, and saplings. If you can learn to recognize the species deer utilize, then all the better, but it's really not necessary. If hunting in heavy timber or brush, look for clearings. Deer congregate in these areas. Old burns, clearcuts, and blowdowns are good places to hunt. In country that receives moderate to heavy hunting pressure, search out places that are missed.

Most hunters often overlook areas that to them just don't look like buck country. Few men want to wander into steep, rugged canyons, let alone drag a deer out of them. These rugged little canyons are often the best bet for a trophy rack. Large bucks will move into such canyons if the surrounding country receives much hunting pressure, and to the nimrod who really wants a trophy buck, these canyons are usually veritable deer havens. Perhaps, in the last analysis, those two words are the key—really want. Muley hunting, like most other worthwhile pursuits, is mostly a matter of being willing to work hard.

Heavy and even buck and yours truly.

11

Bucks In Any Weather

Mark Twain, speaking of springtime weather in New England, once jested he'd "counted 136 kinds of weather inside of four-and-twenty hours." He might just as well have said the same thing about autumn weather in much of mule deer country. As an example, while I was hunting deer on Montana's Buffalo Plateau late one September, weather conditions went from hot and dusty with temperatures in the 70's, to blizzards that dropped two feet of snow and plummeted the mercury to single digits, all within "four-and-twenty hours." In between those extremes were drizzle, fog, wind, sleet, rain, hail, thunder, lightning, and nearly anything else imaginable. Maybe there weren't quite "136 kinds of weather," but it was close.

Hot Weather

In Weber County, Utah, where I've done a lot of buck hunting in the past quarter century (could it really have been that long?!), it's frequently hot and dry during the October hunt. On the other hand, like Twain's New England, it's almost as likely to be cold and snowy. In the West, last summer's drought hung on like a pit bull well into most western deer seasons. It was hot and dry in October on my first deer hunt in Colorado, and it was the same a month later on my last hunt in Wyoming.

In that kind of weather, mule deer naturally enough lay up, move later in the evening, bed down earlier in the morning, and seek dense and cool cover on the north- and east-facing slopes where timber is thicker, since less moisture is lost to evaporation there. Frequently, deer will move down lower on a range nearer to available water, where browse is more plentiful and nutritious. If there's a spring or seep in heavy timber or brush, you can bet it's a good place to find deer, especially if there's a concentration of browse within half a mile. Adult bucks are at their prime from late summer to just before the rut in early November, and may have two inches of tallow over the rump and lower back. Just as a fat man suffers more in the heat, heavy bucks will too, so they'll seek out the coolest places they can find and won't move unless they're forced to. I've even jumped bucks laying in old elk wallows.

The best way to hunt bucks during the sometimes wilting, parched conditions common in early hunts is to first isolate bedding areas. Logically, these will be in cool stands of timber or shady north- and east-facing slopes. Bucks may bed on high, breezy ridges, but only in remote country. They also may bed in inaccessible gorges near water, but even there they'll be in heavy timber. As a rule, there will be a number of fresh rubs near the center of the regular bedding areas and a well-worn trail from that stand of brush to wherever the buck is feeding. Also, as a rule, bucks feed in open areas, since preferred browse grows there, not in timber.

There are two ways to hunt bucks when it's hot and dry and they're bedded in thick trees. The first, and best, is to stillhunt very, very slowly along, or just downwind of, the trail as it goes into timber. Always watch downwind of the path, since that's where old bucks will bed. A second way is to drive the stand. Because of steep terrain, too-large timber stands, or other factors, driving is sometimes impractical. But if you decide to "push" for a big buck, understand that if he's been around for a few hunting seasons, he's apt to be as tricky as any whitetail with equal experience, so don't sell him short. (Actually, what I want to say is that he's likely to be more tricky and unpredictable than the average whitetail because he's not quite so inclined to be high-strung and to panic, but since I'm sensitive to epithets, maybe a parenthetical note will suffice).

Wind

Muleys "hole-up" in windy weather. A hard wind makes deer spooky, since all of their senses, with the exception of sight (which isn't much use in heavy cover), are practically useless. Most hunters I know also hole-up when it's windy, but I've found windy conditions can offer good hunting. If you're still-hunting solo through heavy cover, you'll be able to approach a buck very closely because sounds made by the wind mask your own noises. Driving also works because deer are especially nervous and easy to start. Even an old buck, which normally won't move unless you practically step on him, will jump and run the moment he suspects something amiss.

Heavy Rain Or Snow

Deer seek protection during heavy rain or snow, often in the umbrella cover of conifer stands like spruce, fir, or pine. Such conditions make for very good still-hunting, especially if you know the general area where a buck is bedding. Rain and snow makes walking silent and limits a buck's ability to see and hear. If heavy rains or snows continue for several days, however, deer will eventually ignore it and go about their business. When they do, they'll often feed during the day because of feeding time missed, and because of reduced light intensity caused by cloud cover. Since deer are dawn and dusk feeders anyway, they are naturally more active at lower light levels.

Light Rain Or Mist

During a light rain or mist, mule deer tend to stay out feeding later in the morning and begin feeding earlier in the evening. This is because light intensity is reduced during daylight hours, making it seem like feed time to deer, and the true feeding times are also shorter (it gets dark earlier). Glassing and still-hunting near feeding areas in light rain and mist are the best tactics. A light snow has about the same effect, but since snow is associated with cooler temperatures and deer feed more when it's cold, the effect can be exaggerated.

Fog

One of my favorite times to hunt is during fog. It seems to give muleys confidence, and they move around more freely. Still-hunting is the best tactic at this time, and can be used in the feeding or bedding areas. Even wise, old veteran bucks are more sure of themselves, and when it's foggy and cool it's not uncommon to find a trophy buck out browsing late into the morning. If you're still-hunting in fog, it's best to be familiar with the country so you have a fair idea where deer might be. If you're just stumbling around in strange mountains, you'll be lucky to bump into a buck, and you might even get yourself lost. (The only two times I've been really lost have been in heavy fog.) In the Rockies in autumn, the high country can be fogged-in for days at a time. A hunter can either stay inside next to the cook stove, drinking coffee and waiting out the weather, or he can be still-hunting. I prefer the latter, and have taken several bucks because of this.

Approaching Storm

When a storm front is approaching and the barometric pressure begins to drop, deer will feed heavily. I'm convinced that game, and especially mule deer, know when a storm is approaching, and they come out earlier in the evening and stay out later in the morning in anticipation of feeding time lost while sitting out the storm. Such times are among the best for hunting muley bucks, and effective tactics include glassing and still-hunting along ridges or open slopes where you can see a lot of country, and then making a long stalk. If you're intimately familiar with the place, waiting along trails between feeding and bedding areas works even better. During the storm, mule deer will hole-up in heavy cover. After the storm, particularly if it's been a long and bad one, muleys will go on what might almost be described as a feeding frenzy. They'll be everywhere, and even trophy bucks might be out during midday. This is even more true if it's cold and clear.

Heavy Snow

If the storm has dropped a lot of snow, deer will usually migrate down to lower country. If you catch it right, this weather-induced movement can offer the best trophy hunting imaginable. I've only caught the downward migration twice. The first time was in the mountains west of Big Piney, Wyoming. Just before and after the storm, the foothills were filled with deer moving to low country. In a day and a half I saw about thirty-five good bucks, and took one of the best. Another time in Magpie Canyon in northern Utah, I caught a similar migration and I saw maybe twenty large bucks in a day or so. Here, too, I shot a good one. I often dream of seeing one of these migrations again.

Clear

Humidity, temperature, light intensity, and browse conditions being equal, mule deer will be out and active more during clear weather when they can see farther, since they rely on sight almost as much as antelope or mountain sheep. This seems to contradict my earlier statement that bucks move about more freely in fog. Part of the reason for this is that light conditions in fog are usually reduced to dawn or dusk levels, times deer move anyway, so they feel comfortable then.

Extreme Cold

During extreme cold, say single digit weather, deer will normally be out feeding, since cold weather requires more energy to maintain body temperatures. This is especially true if feeding sites are near bedding cover. When there's even a light wind, however, they'll stay in heavy timber. If it's cold during the rut, bucks may be even more active. Deer may also not start feeding until later in the morning when it begins to warm, so they'll stay out feeding later in the day. In colder, late-season hunts, it's productive to still-hunt and glass feeding areas all day long.

Moonlit Nights

In muley hunting circles in the West, there's a pretty common myth that deer feed more actively on moonlit nights and, as a result, bed down earlier in the morning, usually before first light. Mule deer see so well at night that it makes little difference whether or not there is moonlight. I've seen as many deer feeding on totally dark, even overcast nights, as I have when there was a full moon. Some of the deer were seen on a friend's ranch, and since it wasn't deer season and we didn't have guns in the pickup, spotlighting was perfectly legal. The other observations were made over the years, just driving through deer country at night. Deer also move as much the morning after a moonlit night as they do after a totally dark one. While moonlight, or the lack of it, isn't properly considered weather, it's often a subject of debate among deer hunters, and it just as often influences hunter strategy.

Not to be outdone by Mark Twain, Murray Schwartz, a reclusive tundra rat who lives in a remote cabin in the blacktail country of coastal Alaska, told me he'd seen "at least 100 kinds of weather in a day—all of it bad." Confident of his oneupmanship, Murray gazed complacently at the rain pelting the window as proof.

I'm not sure whether I buy all that, but I know bad weather is relative, and that if done right, there is really no weather that's "bad" for hunting deer.

A non-typical but not-too-big buck bagged after a snowstorm.
(Courtesy of Cheri Flory.)

Trophy
Gallery

12

Stop, Pause, And Start For Bucks

The movement and freedom of still-hunting is very satisfying to a restless hunter. While still-hunting, I drift through the aspens or spruce slowly, straining to see as far ahead as possible in order to detect anything out of the ordinary. I listen for something I won't recognize until I've heard it (and more often than not, it's only a chickadee searching for ant eggs or a whitefooted mouse scampering across dry leaves). I even try to scent a buck. "Drift like smoke," a Shuswap guide once told me. At moments like these, I'm as aware of the environment as I ever get.

The stop, pause, and start method of hunting mule deer is basically an exaggerated form of still-hunting. In regular still-hunting, you move quietly through good deer country, stopping often to look and listen. The idea is to move slowly and quietly enough so that you don't pass deer by. In other words, still-hunting increases your own awareness of what's out there.

In a sense, the stop-pause-start method (or SPS, as I'll call it) also serves to keep the hunter aware, but its main function is to move what's out there and hiding in such a way that the hunter can get a shot. The stages of SPS are more drawn out than those of simple still-hunting.

There's not much argument these days that really big mule deer bucks are normally nocturnal during hunting seasons. In a true wilderness, or during the rut or late seasons, this might not always be the case, but in most country and at most times you and I hunt, it is. In other words, if you want to get a shot at a good buck, nine times out of ten you've got to get him to leave his bed. Along with using your own scent to drive game, tracking, and brushing, the SPS method can be very effective. Over my last three deer seasons, which involved seven deer hunts in three Western states, nearly 50 percent of all adult bucks I've seen were flushed by using the SPS method. The largest buck I've bagged since 1980—a huge, even, and heavy-antlered deer that scored 200 Boone and Crockett points green—was taken using SPS in 1986.

As with any other form of hunting, you don't use SPS just anywhere. Use it in a place where there's a fair chance that a good buck might be hiding, and in a place where if he is flushed, you can get a shot. From my experience, the best places are in ravines or small canyons, geographical features that are blessedly plentiful in mule deer country.

I discovered SPS for myself purely by accident, in a place that I consider even now to be perfectly suited for using it. I'd been walking up a long, steep ravine all morning. The vegetation was sparse on the steep, south-facing slope, with only an occasional thick patch of scrub oak or chokecherry. I'd skipped breakfast and my belly had begun rumbling, so I sat down to eat lunch. Across the ravine was a small patch of oak scrub that stood about chest high. The leaves had fallen and I thought I could see into it pretty well, although at that point I didn't see a thing. After lunch, roughly 40 minutes later, I stood up, fumbled around for a few minutes as I got ready to go (this commotion is often a key element in flushing a buck), and then stepped out. At that moment a good buck bounced from the scrub oak and up the slope. It was an easy matter to collect him on the open hillside.

Another good place to jump bucks using the SPS method is from brush patches located below you but still on the same slope. The idea is to flush the buck onto the opposite slope where you can get a shot. The more open the slope, the better. Canyon heads, brushy or timbered canyon bottoms, isolated stands of timber, and thickets are also good places to employ the SPS method. If you're right and the spot you select does hold a good buck (more often than not it won't—there just aren't that many big bucks), you must be positioned where you're able to get a shot. It doesn't do much good to flush a buck into even thicker brush or timber, or over a ridge where you can't shoot. The best places to use SPS are pockets of brush or timber that are surrounded by relatively open terrain that a fleeing buck must cross. The rule, rather than the exception, is that a buck will be running, so any shooting must be done quickly. If you're hunting perfectly flat terrain, which isn't often the case in mule-deer country, you need at least two hunters. One should wait on either side of the suspicious cover.

Though everything was purely coincidental the day I discovered SPS for myself, all the elements were there. I'd luckily stopped at a likely looking place; I'd paused long enough for the buck to get nervous; and I made a commotion before I left. The commotion, at least in this case, was the kicker.

Stop

In other words, the SPS method involves locating good-looking cover—and stopping. Always make some commotion so that any buck will be aware of your presence (in all likelihood, he probably will be regardless of the noise you make), so he has time to get nervous. Don't make too much of a commotion, since you don't want to frighten bucks any farther up the canyon. Make just enough to catch the attention of any nearby buck.

Pause

The next step, the "pause" stage, is to wait. Don't hide—that defeats your purpose. Remain conspicuous. I usually wait at least 30 minutes or so before starting again unless, for some reason, I'm in a hurry. The pause stage is a good time to eat lunch, meditate, or reminisce about the ones that got away (keeping, of course, one eye on the suspected cover).

Start

The last stage of the SPS method is starting out again. Remember to fiddle around before leaving. This is often the time when a buck will get nervous and flush. I believe this is the point at which the buck is finally convinced he's been located, and once he's convinced of that, he'll run.

I've found the SPS method to be most useful during late mornings and from mid-afternoon until near-dark. The reason for this is that mule deer and most other game I've observed tend to sit tighter the longer they've been bedded, so SPS can be an effective way to move an otherwise complacent buck. A muley that's just bedded down as it starts to get light, on the other hand, is more apt to flush on its own with little provocation from you, lessening the need for SPS.

In the past, I've discovered that bucks are also likely to flush wild at around 1 p.m. The reason, I believe, is that they're thinking of getting up anyway for a quick bite or a stretch or simply to change positions, so SPS is not always effective. This is more true in thick cover than in sparse cover. If a buck beds in sparse cover, he probably plans to stay there until dark, so he'll sit tight.

During mid- and late-afternoon, bucks have usually been bedded for a few hours, so there's little worry that they'll flush wild. This is a good time to use SPS. Be on the safe side, however, since older bucks are unpredictable, and be sure to move quietly until you're ready to use the SPS method. In fact, a hunter should always move cautiously and stalk every suspicious patch of brush or timber as if it hid the biggest and smartest buck around.

In the evening, since it's getting dark and is nearly feeding time, bucks are restless and hungry and are again more apt to sneak away on their own, lessening the need to use the SPS method. Of course, using it can't hurt your chances, either.

Most of the behavior of mule deer I've been talking about so far applies mainly to wise, older, adult bucks. Younger bucks, from yearlings up to say three-and-one-half or even four-and-one half year-olds, often won't be as nocturnal as trophy bucks. They're also more apt to flush quickly from cover. Creating a commotion at the end of the "pause" and beginning of the "start" phase may not be needed, but use it anyway if nothing has flushed. Since they're younger and less experienced, young bucks are easier to bag using not only SPS, but any hunting method.

Though I've reduced the SPS method to three nice, clean, tidy stages, suggested the length of the waiting time, and even specified certain flourishes such as making a commotion in the right places (almost like a play in three acts), for a more accurate picture think of the stages of SPS as rough suggestions.

A large mule deer buck is a clever, cool, fluid, and adaptable animal that will never be taken consistently by using a set of rules or steps. The hunter who can lengthen or shorten the waiting time based on a hunch, or can locate an unlikely cover that holds a buck as a result of some sixth sense, will always be more successful than the hunter who does it by the numbers. A hunter should be as fluid and adaptable as his quarry.

13

Stalking During The Rut

Younger bucks begin rutting early in November. Mature, trophy bucks, however, usually don't begin until about the middle of the month, depending on such factors as temperature, weather and the availability of estrus (in heat or season) does. Generally, mule deer rut a bit earlier if it's cold, and an early or mid-November storm and cold front may be just what's needed to start rutting activity. The rut peaks, again as a rule (we're talking about animals, with wills of their own, not numbers, so there are always exceptions) during the last half of November. It is pretty well finished by the middle of December or so. Desert muleys rut at least a month later in most cases, and as mentioned in another chapter, I've watched mule deer acting rutty into February in Sonora.

The Old Myth

The old myth is that bucks become addled during the rut. And that's exactly what that is, a myth; mature bucks in hunted country stay as secretive and nocturnal as at any other time when hunting season is in progress. Immature bucks, those under 4½ years of age, do become foolish, a bit like high school jocks during their senior year. Trophy bucks do, however, hang around doe groups, and they'll usually show up only after does have begun to come into estrus, or breeding condition. According to my old research as a biologist and my newer research as a trophy buck hunter, this tends to begin about mid-November. Adult bucks will often breed at night, which doesn't help the hunter any, but they will breed during the day, a chink in their armor, if does come into estrus then, especially if there are other, pesky, younger bucks about. Probably the best tactic for getting a trophy buck during the rut is to simply watch big doe groups. I know a spot where a number of does live consistently, year in and year out. Occasionally I hunt with a muzzleloader, and in Utah the season runs through early November, as the rut is getting into swing. I watch the canyon, and if I've got enough time, I know that eventually a good buck is going to show himself, if there's one in the area. Stalking close enough for a shot with the .54 Hawkin replica is another matter entirely.

Moving Closer To Does

During the rut, trophy bucks typically move their "center area" to a location closer to does. Look into (*carefully,* if you don't want to frighten the buck out of the vicinity) ravine and canyon heads where there's thick timber or brush for a concentration of beds (about 4 feet long, with brush and rocks cleared away), rubs (bark scraped from saplings—a big buck usually batters saplings greater than 3 or 4 inches in diameter), droppings, scrapes (bucks paw a hollow and urinate and defecate in it), and other "sign." Also smell for a musky, pungent, rutting odor that you'll probably recognize once you smell it even if you've never scented it before; it's that distinctive. If you're pushed for time, "center areas" are good places to employ very, *very* cautious stillhunting. Wear wool, since you can't get quieter, and if you're wearing leather or rubber boots, cover them with some sort of "quiet" material to muffle the sound of branches scraping against them. Track or stillhunt along one of the trails going into the thick of the tangle, but move as slowly and silently as humanly possible. Keep your rifle at the ready with your thumb on the safety, because if you jump a buck he'll be close and he'll waste no time clearing the area. Don't get discouraged if the buck isn't home; try again a day or two later, since bucks wander a great deal while rutting.

Rattling

Another sometimes effective tactic is rattling two antlers together. Rattling is a new tactic for mule deer hunters; in fact I know of no one that uses it in the U.S. For techniques, see the chapter "Rattlin' Muley Bucks." Rattling doesn't work as well for muleys as it does for whitetails, and it's not as predictably successful as other mule-deer tactics such as stillhunting and its adjunct, the SPS method (see the chapter "Stop, Pause and Start For Bucks"), or even brushing or standing. But under the right conditions, it works surprisingly well. The best place and time to use rattling is in a buck's center area during the rut. While using the technique, I've been nearly run over by several bucks, and have bagged several others at very close range. Several times bucks "roared" at me, thinking I was an interloper into their living room, and a buck's "roar" is an astonishing and intimidating sound.

Rattling also sometimes works near doe groups. I've had bucks trot into the open from stands of aspen or fir the first time I touched antlers together, though mostly these were younger bucks, not the mature, trophy animals you'd likely find in a good center area. On the other hand, it's possible that on those occasions, there just weren't any big bucks in the country, which is becoming the rule rather than the exception in hunted country.

Younger bucks tend to approach your rattling with caution; they tend not to be dominant bucks, and want to see just what the competition is before engaging in battle, or even sparring. The local stud, which *is* dominant, will approach with fire in his eye if you've fooled him with your rattling. In an undisturbed area, there will be one dominant buck which became dominant during prerutting sparring matches. Other bucks in the area tested the stud buck at this time and found they just weren't big and tough enough to beat him in a real fight. This drastically lessens the need for potentially lethal battles farther along in the rut, since bucks know they can't beat the stud buck, so why try?

Look For "Sign"

If you're strickly out for a trophy buck, make sure there's one in the area by looking for big buck sign (large tracks, rubs, scrapes). Undoubtedly you will find big buck sign if there's one in the area; typically trophy bucks make a long circuit periodically, visiting various doe groups, and in doing so, leave sign all over the place.

As stated earlier, big bucks don't get more foolish while rutting, so forget that myth. Unlike myriads of rumors to the contrary, trophy bucks don't get stupid because they have love on the brain. In fact, if you're pressed for time, bagging a good buck during the rut is going to be hard. Bucks during the rut move around more, mostly at night, and they're tougher to pinpoint at a given time. When your time is running out, stillhunt, track or rattle— tactics designed to make something happen. If you've go more time, than wait around a doe herd. Bucks *are* predictable during the rut, and eventually they *will* show up in a doe group.

Buck following the scent of a doe in heat (estrus).

Buck exhibiting "flehmen" or "lip curl."

This buck is making a scrape—defecating and urinating in a hoofed-out depression.

14

The Art Of Tracking

The big muley buck moved down off a heavily timbered slope and onto the rolling sagebrush hills. I had been watching him with binoculars from half a mile away. He moved purposefully in the pre-dawn half-light, silhouetted against the new snow, his neck swollen with rut. Then he was gone, disappearing into one of the brush-choked ravines.

I shivered, slipped the binoculars back into my coat, and headed toward where I had last seen the big buck. The light was coming fast when I cut his track. He was following another deer, one whose track was much smaller than his; a doe near estrus, I reasoned. I followed the trail.

A mile farther down the ravine, the buck had caught up with the doe. Their tracks milled about in the sagebrush, then continued. The doe was still leading, and judging by her unceasing pace and obvious restlessness, she was probably very nearly in season. The buck would stay with her until she was bred or a bigger buck chased him off. Several hours later they began to meander, looking for a place to bed. They had been quartering into the icy November wind.

The tracks angled out of the ravine, up onto a flat, and then along the edge of the ravine back toward where they had come from. They had bedded momentarily on a bluff overlooking the ravine before catching my scent. I scanned the open country. Well out of rifle range, the buck and doe were climbing the opposite slope of a big draw that was almost a canyon.

The deer had beaten me with probably the most common trick hunted mammals use. They circled downwind of their trail so that anything following would have to approach from upwind. I was new to hunting then, but it was not the first time I had made that mistake. And it would not be the last. But it was the first time I realized that there was more than just bad luck involved each time a buck escaped by winding me.

Looping

It was several years later before I was introduced to the "loop method" (mentioned earlier) by a Shuswap Indian in British Columbia. The method was so simple I was amazed I hadn't thought of it before. You simply determine the quarry's direction and the wind direction and then loop downwind of the trail. The end of each loop will cut the track. If the end of the last loop passes the trail, make smaller loops back toward where you last saw tracks.

I first tried the method for myself while hunting elk in Montana's Absaroka-Beartooth Wilderness. I had spent a week of pre-season scouting and nearly a week of hunting and had not seen a trophy bull. There was a band of yearling bulls, four-points, and one medium-sized five-point hanging out in a·basin below Iron Mountain. Time was getting short, so I decided to forget the trophy and go for meat.

The bulls had bedded on a steep talus slope until the light snow had quit sometime early in the morning, then moved along a thickly timbered ledge into Hummingbird Creek. I jumped the bulls on a point above the creek. Several rushed through the lodgepole pine below me back along the ledge, while others dropped straight off into the canyon. Two, from their tracks the largest, headed along a timbered slope up the canyon. I knew it was no use to follow their tracks in the heavy timber and that if they did stop they would be alert and watching their back trail, so I headed into the canyon bottom and up the opposite slope and then up the canyon. Above, in a broad basin, I circled back toward where I thought the bulls would go if they continued. But there were no tracks coming out of the timbered slope. The bulls were still below.

I looped toward where I had last seen the elk a mile below, staying downwind of where I thought they might be. I cut their trail at the end of the second loop. I made the loops smaller and followed the trail, staying downwind of it. The wind was coming up the slope, at right angles to the trail, so it was easy to follow it and still stay downwind. The bulls had meandered through the timber and were, from their tracks, looking for a place to bed. They intended to be both downwind and within sight of their backtrail. All of my senses were at full alert. I was sure the bulls were very near.

Then there was a movement ahead and slightly below. Perhaps it had been a squirrel. I stared hard into the shadows. The brown branches of a blowdown gradually became the forelegs of an elk. Then I could see an ear twitch, searching for whatever had alerted it, and then an antler tine. The bull stepped

The "Loop Method" of tracking. The hunter loops downward of the buck's trail, returning periodically for confirmation he's still on it. If he passes the end of the trail, he makes smaller loops back in the direction where he last cut the trail.

closer, trying to identify the danger, and as he did so I settled my crosshairs on the red neck mane that had momentarily appeared in an opening. I shot and the five-point bull was dead.

Old And New Tracks

The "loop" and other methods of tracking are effective only if the tracks are reasonably fresh. If you've seen the animal, then obviously they are fresh. But if you haven't, it can sometimes be difficult to determine just how old a track might be.

I learned this while following a large moose track along the mud of an arctic river for nearly four miles. It meandered in and out of the willow flats and flood channels, and I expected to see the bull at any moment. It was a beautiful Indian summer day. Chevrons of snow and Canada geese honked and cackled overhead as they winged south. The willows and dwarf poplars along the river had turned to gold, and the sun hanging low in the southern sky was pleasantly warm on my back. From time to time caribou would swim the river heading southeast toward their wintering grounds. I had already taken a good caribou bull and was happy just to watch them for a while.

Then the track climbed out of the bottom onto a sandy, eight-foot bluff and continued along the river. In the sandy soil the tracks were only nondescript depressions. A little farther on, I jumped a cow and calf moose that had been feeding in the willows, and examined their tracks. I could see every detail. I was amazed. The moose tracks I had been following were several days, maybe a week old. They had appeared fresh only in the mud and damp soil along the river.

Rain and frost can help determine if tracks are fresh. If there are depressions from raindrops in the track, it was made before or during the last rain, whether it was an hour or a week ago. If there are no rain prints in the track, it was made since the last rain. Tracks in moist soil are quickly obliterated by frost action. When moisture in the soil freezes it expands, distorting and erasing. All but the very driest soil is affected by frost.

On dry soils, wind plays a big part in aging tracks. The only way to tell for certain in any given area is to make a few tracks and note their change in the next few hours, and in the next few days.

I once spent several fruitless days in northern Sonora trying to get close enough to a large desert ram for some photos. One morning as I wandered up a slightly damp arroyo, I came upon what appeared to be very large and very fresh sheep tracks.

I followed them out of the wet sand in the arroyo bottom and up a gravelly hill. The sun was heavy away from the coolness of the arroyo and the shade of the paloverde. The tracks angled up the slope in the gravel and heat toward a saddle a mile above. As I approached the saddle, the winds picked up. I was aware of the wind only because it felt so good as it cooled me in my sweat-soaked shirt. There was a fine sand in the saddle and the tracks were only slight depressions when they were present at all. I remembered how I had been fooled before by old tracks that looked fresh in mud or damp soil.

Hot and thirsty, and a little disgusted with myself, I headed toward camp. I turned back quickly to the tinkle of sliding shale in time to see great, rough horns extending on either side of a bony rump as a huge ram disappeared around the curve of the slope. He had been watching me from 30 yards away. I had thought the nearly obliterated tracks in the saddle were old, but the wind, blowing the fine soil, was the culprit.

Interpreting "Sign"

On the springy, trackless tundra (found in rocky country such as sheep and goat habitat) and in some deer country, following an animal by his track is all but impossible. But it is possible to determine whether or not game is present by sign. Sign includes droppings, browsed or grazed plants, wallows, beds, and saplings barked by antler polishing. The hunter can, with practice, even find out when and where game feeds or beds.

I'd been hunting moose on some rolling tundra hills above the Arctic Circle for several days and had not seen a bull. In the small ravines there were willows and dwarf poplar, favorite moose browse, as well as a few stunted spruce. Except in the mud where migrating caribou had crossed muskeg or streams, the country would not take a hoofprint. The tundra was trackless and would spring back into place after a foot was lifted.

Since I wasn't having any luck close to camp I moved farther away. In a small gully several miles from camp I found where a bull had battered an 8-foot spruce (at that latitude, perhaps a 300-year-old tree) with his antlers. Nearby, the willows and poplars had been browsed heavily. Where the shoots had been freshly cropped, the pulpy fibers were cream color. The older the cropping, the browner the fibers. Shoots that were gray at the cut were very old, perhaps from the preceding winter. There were many freshly browsed willows. I moved up the ravine. There was a concentration of droppings and a place where the tundra grasses had been crushed flat. A few of the grasses were trying to spring back upright. The bull had just left his bed. I hoped he had not scented or heard me. I had been quiet and was sure the wind had been favorable all the way up the ravine. As I stood up from examining the bed there was a rustle in the 10-foot scrub and a massive bull stepped into the open 10 yards away. I dropped him with a shot to the neck. The bull had a 64-inch spread with long, many-pointed palms, and was my best Alaskan moose.

Dry, rocky country poses similar problems. Once, hunting the Dolores River country of western Colorado, I'd gone for several days without so much as seeing a decent buck. Following the advice of Bud Hendrickson, on whose ranch I'd been hunting, and a hunch of my own, I changed tactics. Instead of working the mesa tops and arroyos near the river, I would go high into the cliffs and talus slopes along the Uncompahgre Plateau.

I had spent the morning working around the base of a large cliff that topped off a small, but steep, mountain. In most of the country it was essentially trackless rock, cliff, and talus. Late in the morning I found where a buck had polished his antlers on a gnarled old willow growing out of a moist seep in the rocks. The rub was not too old and a few drops of sap were running slowly down the scar.

A little farther on there was a freshly scraped bed at the base of a massive monolith. The shale and soil were still damp from the recent scraping. There was a single large track in the soil near the center of the bed. I knew then there was a good buck hanging out somewhere in the rocks and ledges. Still farther on there was a pile of droppings on a broad ledge. While the pellets on top of the pile were cool, those on the bottom retained some heat. I reasoned the droppings would cool quickly in the cold November air, so the buck must have passed by only a short while earlier. I moved up the ledge, occasionally peeking over the cliff to the talus slope below. The ledge widened and opened into a chute filled with aspen saplings, mountain mahogany, and bitterbrush—favorite deer browse. I sat down on a rock on the edge of the chute, trying to decide how best to hunt it. There was a movement in the dwarf aspen across the chute. I put the binoculars on the large, dark body of a deer trying to hide. After a few moments I could discern antlers through the leafless branches. I worked a cartridge into the chamber and quickly the buck was off, downhill. I swung ahead of him and when he cleared the screen of brush, squeezed. The buck crumpled, slid a few yards on the talus, and lay still. Though not a monstrous trophy, he was a good, mature, and very fat, four-pointer.

Know Behavior

In country that does take a track, it is helpful to know a little about the behavior of the species you're hunting. If the track is traveling in a straight line, and especially if it is running or trotting, the game is probably moving out of the country and it will do little good to follow it. Much caribou hunting is done somewhere along a particular herd's migration route. The animals are always on the move and following their trail is a waste of time and effort. I know, because I tried it.

Other animals may leave the country if they are badly frightened. This is particularly true of elk. If they are spooked they may travel 10, 20, or more miles before they feel they are safe.

A big, smart muley buck may also put several miles between himself and hunters when thoroughly frightened. The same is often true for grizzly and, occasionally, for black bear.

Meandering Or Circling Tracks

Meandering or circling tracks may mean different things, depending upon the species hunted. In wild ungulates—deer, elk, moose, and sheep—a meandering or circling trail usually means the animal is looking for a place to bed. These animals will almost always bed where they can hear, see, or smell anything approaching on their backtrail. Sheep rely most on their sense of sight, so they normally bed or rest in a place that commands a wide view of the surrounding country, such as at the tops of cliffs or points along a ridge. Pronghorns also rely primarily on eyesight, and in areas where they are heavily hunted, they have an uncanny ability to judge effective rifle range. A mule deer may also rely heavily on eyesight, depending upon terrain, and often will bed on a bare knoll or along a ridge to watch the surrounding country. Whitetails, moose, mule deer, and elk in timber will bed downwind of their backtrail. Bears also rely heavily on scent. All game animals seem to be alert to strange, out-of-place sounds such as brush scraping against stiff fabrics, the metallic sounds of a bolt ramming a cartridge into the chamber, or the clink of keys in a hunter's pocket.

Natural sounds, such as branches breaking or rocks rolling or splashing, if not carried to the extreme, usually won't spook game that's not already wary, though they may put the quarry on alert. What does send an animal on its way is the unnatural sound.

Circling by dangerous game may mean something completely different than it does when a deer or sheep is involved. If the animal knows it is being followed or if it is wounded, it may be circling to ambush the tracker. Once, armed with only a camera, I had located an unusually blond grizzly a mile down a ridge from where I'd been photographing Dall rams. I decided to try for the bear and spent much of the rest of the day following it through thick tangles of willow and poplar or through stands of spruce. Several times I had a strong hunch the grizzly knew I was following it. It was not feeding as bears normally would be doing in preparation for the long winter. Though it was not running, it had several times circled downwind of its backtrail.

Toward later afternoon, to my relief, the bear moved out of thick brush and up the open channel of a meandering glacial river. I followed the tracks a mile or more up the riverbed before something made me turn around. The bear emerged from the willow and poplar scrub along the river, waded the main channel, picked up my scent trail and began following it. He had circled downwind and waited until I passed; then, perhaps a bit tired of the game, had turned the tables. Now I was the hunted. I searched frantically for a tree to climb. There wasn't one. I climbed up a slight rise and figured that, come what may, I might as well take photos. The closer the bear got and the fresher my scent, the more the hackles on his neck, shoulders, and head would rise. I was resigned to the fact that I was about to be mauled. I remembered the things one should do under such circumstances—play dead, protect the back of the neck and the crotch—all the while clicking photos of the approaching bear. When the grizzly got within 50 yards he broke into a gallop, heading straight for me. He stopped at 20 feet, growled menacingly a few times, then, to my vast relief, walked off.

Though my interest in reading spoor came about as a way to improve hunting success, I now often pursue it for its own sake. There are few things more agreeable than tracking an elk or muley buck in the first heavy snows of December, long after the hunting seasons have closed, or a grizzly or moose during the off-season in Alaska. There is a great deal of satisfaction in knowing when a buck or bull had passed and what he was doing. And the practice of reading spoor sharpens a hunter's skill as nothing else can.

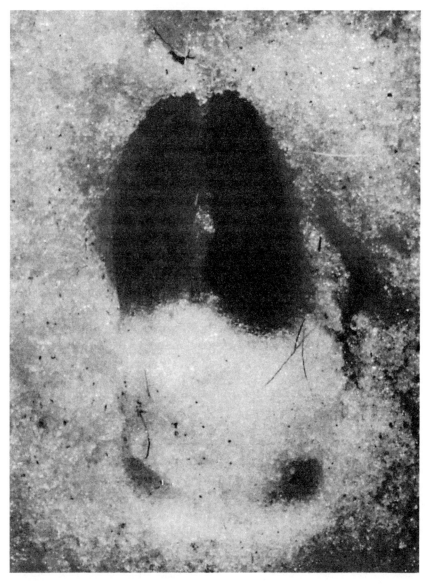

A buck track. The main hoof print is 3 ¾ inches long, excluding dew claws. Note the dew claws and hair.

15

Rattlin' Muley Bucks

About twenty years ago, back when I was starting my research as a biologist on elk behavior, I noticed bulls sparred frequently just before the rut. At first, I kept data, as I was supposed to do, but since I was also an elk hunter, I brought some small, rag-horn antlers into the field and tried to rattle some bulls in. I was in Yellowstone at the time, and within a week I'd rattled in thirteen bulls. It was mid-September. Bulls were getting rutty and testing each other and themselves by putting their antlers together and shoving each other about almost playfully. Sparring, and the effectiveness of antler rattling, falls off when the rut gets into full swing, and for elk that's about September 21 in an average year (whatever that is!).

Nearly fifteen years later, I watched two whitetail bucks spar in a river bottom of southern Montana. The bucks had been at it for twenty minutes when I noticed another one trotting down the creek through patches of willows toward them. I was startled to see it was a mule deer. The revelation hit as hard as if I'd just had the meaning of life unfold before me. *Why not!?* I asked myself.

Before that time, I'd never considered rattling for mule deer, probably because I'd never seen anything mentioned in biological literature and partly because I'd read several hunting "experts" say it couldn't be done. It's true that mule deer aren't as easily rattled as whitetails or moose, but at certain times and under certain conditions, it can be effective.

All antlered game put their antlers together and shove. Mostly, this is just sparring—a behavior that strengthens neck muscles, develops timing and coordination, releases increasing libido and aggression as the rut approaches, and sizes up the competition in the valley, thereby making it unnecessary for potentially lethal battles later on. Once in a while, members of the deer family do fight. Here, the encounter is more intense, the action more rapid, and animals are sometimes seriously injured or even killed. Mule deer seem to fight less often than whitetails, elk or moose—in thirty years as a deer hunter (I started when I was 13) and twenty as a biologist, I've only witnessed four bonafide mule deer battles. One was in the volcanic mountains of northern Sonora, Mexico; two were in Yellowstone not far from Tower Junction; and the fourth was near Waterton Park in Alberta. All except one lasted more than three minutes, and in one fight the buck lost an eye. In that period of time, I've seen over three-hundred sparring matches. When you rattle for muleys, then, you're trying to bring a buck in for sparring. Bucks spar most frequently just before the rut. Even big, stud bucks will spar then if there are other bucks around of nearly equal size. Small bucks may engage antlers with a big buck briefly, but they soon disengage and scamper off.

Thrashing (scraping and smashing brush with an antler) can work as well as rattling. It's more effective than rattling during the rut, roughly from mid-November through early December, because trophy breeding bucks have by then already sized up the competition and there's no need for further sparring to decide who's boss; if they put antlers together during the rut, it's usually to fight.

Pre-rut

When rattling during the pre-rut (September through early November), don't do it too intensely. Hard clattering and vigorous, quick smashing of antlers indicates a fight, and since bucks don't fight during the pre-rut, it hints something's wrong to a buck. He'll go in the opposite direction. Instead, bring the antlers together lightly at first, and not too frequently. Just touch the tips together, since you don't want to frighten a buck that may be nearby. After ten minutes of this, rattle more loudly so the sound carries greater distances, but don't do it too vigorously or too often, which again would indicate higher levels of aggression in real bucks. Since I'm still experimenting and learning, I can't say with certainty just how long you should rattle before moving on. I one time had a buck come to my rattling an hour after I'd started it. Usually, though, I only rattle half an hour at one place, then circle into the wind and find another spot. The distance I move before I rattle again depends on wind conditions (sound is muffled in the wind), whether there's running water nearby (this, too, drowns antler clattering) and terrain (sound doesn't carry as far in thick coniferous forests). I almost invariably circle into the wind, since I don't want my scent to get to a buck before my rattling does.

During the pre-rut, antler rattling is best for smaller bucks because they're less cautious than wise, veteran bucks that tend to be mostly nocturnal in hunted country. It's easier to rattle in two- or three-year-olds—good meat but no trophy—than it is to get a mature buck. This is especially true in the open. Adult bucks can be rattled in, but I've only done it in the "center area" of their home range (some writers call this the "core area," but since that term has been used to define a number of different concepts, I'll use "center area," a term I first used in the early seventies). You can find a big buck's center area by tracks (an adult buck's fore-hoof is 3½-4 inches long), rubs, scrapes (yes, mule deer do rub and scrape, though for different reasons than whitetails), beds, droppings, and cropped feed plants. Center areas are almost always in thick brush or timber, often near a canyon head where all a buck has to do is step over the ridge to be in a different drainage. They're also common in large stands of timber or brush; there, the buck just runs into more cover without ever having to cross the open.

To rattle in a large buck's center area successfully, you've got to get there quietly, and this means moving silently (wear "quiet" clothing and soft-soled footgear, and stalk slowly), stalking into the wind, and staying to cover so the buck can't see you. It's best to sneak along the game trail between feeding and bedding areas, since there's less brush and it's easier to move quietly. I once tried rattling in the center area of what from track size seemed to be a good buck's home range. I'd found shed antlers earlier in the day (actually, sheds are normally too dry for rattling), and almost as an afterthought, I sat down near several beds and clattered the antlers lightly. I heard a very definite "roar" (mule deer do indeed roar, I've had half a dozen do it to me, and it sounds nearly like a grizzly or angry mother moose; it's a scary sound in close when you don't know what it is!); then, more quickly than the time it takes to read this line the buck crashed out of brush and nearly ran over me. I was so startled and it happened so suddenly, I didn't get a shot. The buck whirled around in thick brush just below, roared again, then caught my scent and crashed off down the slope. That was the first time I'd rattled in an adult buck, though I'd rattled up a number of smaller ones. The next time, I was ready. I'd found the buck's center area, had sneaked into it without being detected, and lightly touched the antler tips together. Almost immediately I heard something in a chokecherry thicket just above, and the buck stepped out. He was hidden by fir boughs, but I could see legs and rump, and from these I knew he was a "shooter." I eased the rifle up and thumbed off the safety. The buck stepped into the open and I pressed the trigger. He was a good, adult buck with nicely formed antlers and five points to the side.

I've also brought both small and big bucks in by smashing an antler against brush. It's best with fresh (not dry or shed) antlers against dry brush so sound carries. For a big buck, it's also best in the center area. Only younger bucks, from yearlings to, say, three-and-a-half-year-olds, will come to rattling or thrashing in the open during the pre-rut.

Rut

During the rut, adult breeding bucks almost never spar with other bucks. Their aggression levels are high, and sparring turns into fighting. They also already know who the competition is, and younger bucks are smart enough not to bother the old stud. The only time a fight may occur is when a stranger buck of nearly equal size appears. As a result of decreasing sparring, rattling isn't as effective during the rut. Antler thrashing of brush is, though, at least in a big buck's center area or around places does feed.

Adult bucks during the rut make rounds that may cover an area that is much larger than their normal home ranges (the center area is only a small part of the home range). Does congregate where there's good, easily available feed and cover. Rattling works well near these places for small bucks, but seldom for larger ones. Thrashing dried brush with an antler seems to work, on the other hand. Last season during the Utah muzzle-loading hunt, I thrashed some aspen deadfall with an antler. Two nearby does took alarm and trotted into the quakies. Then there was a commotion just up the slope, and a decent buck trotted into view. He was too far for a shot with the .54 Hawkin, so I thrashed the brush again, this time softly. The buck looked my way, then walked into some aspens in a small ravine that led down toward where I was hidden. After maybe five minutes, I thrashed the brush again, vigorously at first, then not quite so hard. The buck trotted onto an open slope fifty yards away and stared hard in my direction. I had the buck solid in my sights, touched the set trigger . . . and he just stood there staring after the cap went off. The gun had misfired! I fiddled with the nipple, fitted another cap, and still the buck stood looking at me. It misfired again, and the buck trotted off. The last I saw of him was those 5 x 5 antlers disappearing over a ridge as I cursed fluently. During the rut, places where does feed and bed are good areas to watch and thrash near.

Post-rut

After the rut, some bucks may begin to spar again. I've found this more true of moose and elk. Usually, though, hunting seasons are pretty well finished by the time the rut winds to a close in mid-December or so. If there are still late hunts going, rattling may work again. It won't be as good as during the pre-rut, because after the rut, bucks, especially breeders, are pretty well worn down and don't waste too much energy pushing each other around—but it should work since I've watched several small bucks sparring then. I haven't actually rattled bucks up late in the season, but if my experiences with moose and elk are any indication, it's at least theoretically probable. The difference here between moose and elk, and mule deer, is that muleys don't finish rutting until well into December, which may be full-winter and a time when feeding is critical for survival. Next year I'll have to get out and try to rattle muleys in late December, just to see if it works.

When rattling for mule deer, placement of the "hide" is critical. Always rattle downwind of where you expect the buck to approach. Timing of rattles is important, too. I rattle (clash) the antlers lightly two or three times, pause for four or five minutes, do it again, pause again for the same period of time, try it once more, then wait for maybe ten minutes. Then, I rattle harder so the sound carries farther, but I keep the same cadence. I learned this from sparring matches I'd observed with two and three-year-old bucks. It's my opinion that rattling may work better just after a cold snap or snowstorm, just before the rut gets a full head of steam. I know it does for moose.

Rattling may not be a panacea for mule deer hunters. Tracking and stillhunting, and possibly even driving or "standing" may be more fruitful tactics for big mule deer. On the other hand, with more practice, more field observation and more study, rattling for mule deer may indeed become a panacea. The jury's still out, at least as far as I'm concerned. But either way, it's one more trick in a hunter's day-pack, and when other tactics fail, rattling may be just the one that hangs a buck on the game pole.

16

Trophy Buck Cover

Back when I was a graduate student studying wildlife biology, I learned that along with food and water, cover was a basic requirement of all animals. Hunted animals, like mule deer, use cover for protection and escape, and each cover type is used at different times and for different conditions.

Protection

Mule deer, and man, use cover to get out of the weather. They head for the trees during a storm (man heads for a tent or home), and they'll go for shade if it's hot. It it's too windy on a ridge, bucks will go down into the trees, brush, or to lee of rocks.

In remote mule deer country, bucks are concerned with cover mainly as protection from the elements. This may not be the case if there are wolves or cougars around. They may bed any place out of wind, sun, or snow, though often this offers little protection from man, the predator and hunter. Many times I've seen mature bucks bed in small tangles of shintangle pine, fir, aspen or other brush that was completely surrounded by open country, and when I "jumped" the buck, it was a cinch to hit him as he bounded off.

Bucks seek heavy cover when it's windy, and they'll usually leave smaller patches of brush on open slopes and ridges. On windy days, stillhunting through stands of timber is the best tactic. An advantage the buck stalker has on windy days is that the sound of the wind will mask most small noises he makes. On the other hand, bucks will be more spooky because they can't hear approaching danger until it's on them; often they'll flee with almost no provocation.

When it's raining or snowing hard, bucks will also head into thick trees, particularly conifers, since these have thicker and evergreen foliage which provides better protection than leafless deciduous trees. Dampness from rain and snow make stillhunting relatively easy, since it's not hard to be quiet, and deer tend to be much calmer than during a wind storm. When stalking in the woods, shooting will always be quick and close. Keep your gun ready, a cartridge in the chamber, your thumb on the safety, and stay fully alert all the time. Always stalk into the wind, if at all possible, and avoid unnatural noises such as the scrape of brush against stiff fabric. Whenever it's storming, hunt the woods.

Escape

The hunting most trophy buck hunters does won't be in wilderness. Too often there will be other redshirts in the area, or at least across the canyon, and big bucks will be *alert*. Under such conditions, adult bucks will bed in thick brush or timber—escape cover, in other words. Escape cover is usually large so a buck can run deeper into it. It will be thick, and tough for a predator to move through without being detected by the buck.

Adult bucks don't hang out in the open during hunting season, unless a buck has been sampling hallucinogenic mushrooms. They hole up in the thickest tangle they can find (adult bucks' center areas are invariably in thick tangles), and they won't move into the open during daylight. Occasionally bucks bed at the "edge" of the open and cover, invariably into the cover a few feet or yards. If hunters appear, they simply melt back into the trees. In hunted country, bucks do not normally hide in small patches of cover, no matter how thick, if they must cross open terrain to escape, so keep to big stands of timber and brush.

Obviously, you've go to stalk through thick escape cover without the buck sensing you. Therefore, wear "quiet" wool, try to hunt into the wind, move slowly (both for silence, and so you sense anything there before it senses you), and watch carefully ahead and to the sides. Don't look for the entire animal, since you're only going to spot a piece of him in thick trees. Carefully scan for anything that doesn't quite belong. Above all, don't rush, and I can't say this too often. I've taken full days to stalk through a stand of Douglas fir or lodgepole pine or aspen a mile or so across; that's moving slowly! I read the tracks, and tested the droppings for freshness. If they're warm, they're fresh. The ease with which they crush between thumb and forefinger, and their residual moisture, both indicate degree of freshness. I've also noted their beds, and scrapes. These things told me what the buck was doing, where he was doing most of it, the likelihood of catching him at it at a given time, his size, and how rutty he was. I remember one particular instance that happened in Sheepherd Canyon in Utah. I'd spent two days working a long stand of Douglas fir on a northfacing slope, stalking slowly, being thorough, trying to find a big buck that I knew was there from all his fresh sign or spoor. I had time, so I didn't rush things and risk spooking him out of the country, which is what in all probability would have happened if I'd jumped him in a place where I couldn't get a shot.

The third day, late in the morning, I found droppings that were still warm in the center of the pile, and since the temperature was only in the upper 20s, I knew the pile would cool quickly, and I knew that this one was *fresh*. I followed the tracks in the fir needle-covered loam, a foot at a time. I'd take a step or three, then stop and scan very slowly all of the surrounding forest, looking under blowdowns, through fir boughs, as far away as I could see in the heavy woods. I tested the wind each time I stopped, too, dropping a pinch of dried pine needle duff that would drift off in any slight breeze. Mostly the wind was quiet, or favorable, so I concentrated mainly on being silent and searching through the trees with my eyes. I found the buck bedded behind a blowdown, spotting his antlers sticking up a few inches above the lighter, weathered log. I didn't have a shot at that position, but I had the advantage of surprise. I eased to the left, and down the slope a few feet, watching carefully where I stepped and for any branches that might scrape against my gun or boots. Finally, his neck came into view, and one shot killed him at 16 measured feet.

Stillhunting or tracking through timber is as involving a method of hunting as you'll find. It's mentally exhausting, too, and if you've spent a day stalking slowly through the timber, you'll sleep like deadfall.

17

Return For A Trophy

As we neared the end of a fruitless hunt, the Saskatchewan whitetail guide, as a last resort, agreed to take me to what he termed his "honey hole." We hadn't had any luck in a week of hunting, but he was positive we could take a good buck from his secret spot. As it turned out, he was right.

Over the years, I've found half a dozen mule deer honey holes. One was on a steep ridge in Nevada's Ruby Mountains; another was in a place called Mill Canyon in northern Utah. Probably the best spot was on a high plateau near the Wyoming-Utah border.

Over the past decade I bagged nine adult bucks there, two of which scored near the Boone and Crockett minimum—one just under and one just over. In this area there is abundant feed (bitterbrush, cliffrose, wild rose, gramaniformes, and a variety of palatable forbs); plenty of bedding and escape cover; scattered springs, seeps, and creeks; and until recently, little hunting pressure. Many of the bigger bucks in that country had a long "cheater" point (a single, odd point of an inch or more on an otherwise typical rack) growing halfway up the right antler. There were few does and fawns there, so the buck-to-doe ratio was high.

In short, that plateau had all the right qualities to produce a big buck. The area got little hunting pressure and had some fairly inaccessible places for bucks to retreat to when it did get hunted. There were thick stands of timber for bedding cover on the north and east slopes of the plateau, and apparently the soil quality had the right kinds of minerals to produce big antlers. The soil was also dark and rich in organic matter, which in turn held more moisture and grew bigger and better vegetation. Some sagebrush plants grew 14 feet tall, and one scrub oak tree was 2½ feet in diameter. And perhaps most important, the plateau had the right kind of genetic pool—as evidenced both by the large antler size and the high proportion of bucks with that cheater on the right side. I've killed three bucks with that cheater point in exactly the same place, and I've seen five or six others with it, which means that there were an awful lot of related bucks there.

One good way to find a mule deer honey hole is to locate a place that has consistently produced good bucks in the past. Unfortunately, this isn't as easy as it might seem. One way to locate a prime area is to study the data gathered by game agency checking stations. Many stations collect information on kill location. Another way is to go over back issues of the local newspaper, since a surprising number of papers print stories about particularly large deer taken in local mountains. A third way to sleuth out a good place is to interview hunters in the local gun club or Ducks Unlimited chapter. Perhaps less reliable, but certainly more entertaining, is talking with people in local honky-tonks. Look for taverns that have a number of deer mounts hanging on the walls, but don't believe everything you hear.

Too Many Hunters

As often as not, you're not going to find a place that consistently produces big bucks. Too frequently these days, a muley honey hole doesn't last long because others find out about it, and big bucks either move out or don't survive if their range is heavily hunted. As an example, in Mill Canyon I bagged four good bucks in four consecutive seasons, but during my last successful hunt in that area, I was packing out a buck with a 32-inch spread when I noticed three hunters working a slope upcanyon. The following year, there were half a dozen hunters in the place and I didn't see a decent buck. A season later, the canyon was overrun with redshirts, and to my knowledge, that 32-incher was the last adult buck taken out of the place.

A more famous example occurred in southeastern Utah's once-famed "Triangle." During the late 1950's and '60's, the Triangle (formed by the Colorado border on the east, the Dolores River on the south, and the Colorado River on the northwest) was noted for real trophies. Word got out, hunters swarmed into the red rimrock country, and before long the trophies were gone.

Environmental Change

Another factor that prevents areas from consistently producing trophy bucks is a change in the environment. Occasionally, muley habitat changes because of natural factors, such as last summer's drought. Too often, however, habitat is altered because man constructs a powerline through remote country making it more easily accessible, or roads and trails are pushed into wild lands by agencies such as the Forest Service or BLM.

Sometimes it's better to hunt in a place where one big buck was bagged in the last season or two. It's possible that the buck was just a genetic freak, or one that wandered in from some other range, but it's likely that the big buck was there for a reason. And since he may have been the first trophy buck taken in the area, word probably hasn't gotten out yet and the spot won't be overrun by hunters. Furthermore, since the buck was taken only a year before, the odds are short that the habitat will have changed.

High Buck-to-doe Ratio

Also, look for places that have a high buck-to-doe ratio. Trophy bucks just don't spend their time with pesky fawns and nagging does, unless, of course, it happens to be during the rut in late November or early December. It's a pretty safe bet that if there are a lot of does in the country, there won't be many, if any, good bucks. Adult bucks simply aren't found in places with a high deer density. Be thankful for areas with high deer populations, however, because they lure hunters away from buck honey holes.

A muley buck must survive at least five years to achieve trophy proportions, and most bucks aren't really noteworthy unless they are at least six or seven years old. Of the sixty or so adult bucks I've taken in six states and one Canadian province in the last twenty-seven years, all have been between five and nine years of age. Even under completely natural conditions, it's tough for a buck to survive half a dozen years, and it's next to impossible with myriads of hunters afield. Again, muley honey holes will only be found in places that don't get a great deal of hunting pressure. At times it's very possible to find a good trophy hotspot simply by examining USGS topo maps. If a country has no roads or maintained trails into it, and adjacent places support mule deer, that place may be well worth a try.

"Sign"

Once you're in a suspected honey hole, look for buck "sign." For instance, an adult buck's forehoof measures about 3½ inches in length, and nearly 3 inches in width. Keep in mind the fact that just like people, bucks' feet vary in size. Bucks rub saplings and small trees often, particularly as the rut approaches. During most deer seasons, big bucks will rub trees that are 4 inches in diameter and larger, and the rubs will be fresh. Those made while bucks were clearing their antlers of velvet in early September will often be in open country and dry to the touch. The wetter the rub and the more sap dribbling from it, the fresher it is.

Most buck rubs will be in or near what I call the buck's "center area," the place where big bucks spend virtually all daylight hours. From the center area, there will be at least one well-worn trail leading to one or more feeding areas. These trails are used primarily at night. If the country gets little hunting pressure, it's often productive to wait along the feeding trails early and late in the day. Otherwise, you can stillhunt into the center area along one of the trails if you're careful.

Always watch downwind of the trail, since that's where trophy bucks bed, and also, look for their beds. These are places that have been pawed clear of pebbles and sticks and are about four feet in length. Frequently there will be several within a small area, and the beds will be within a few yards of several rubbed trees. If you spot such a set-up, look around carefully, and put your thumb on the safety. A buck may jump at any moment. If there is plenty of small- and medium-sized deer sign, however, look elsewhere. There probably won't be any good bucks there.

Trophy bucks on good lands normally have a small home range, usually less than 1 mile in diameter and sometimes much less. They spend most of their time in the center area, which may be only 100 yards or so in diameter. Muley bucks normally have only one or two preferred feeding places, and don't wander very much from them. The more a buck wanders, the less familiar he'll be with the terrain, and big bucks like to know exactly where they are. So the chances of taking a big buck in the same place that you or someone else bagged one the preceding season are good. Big bucks aren't nomads; they get big by finding a small area that fulfills all their requirements and staying there. If a buck is bagged in such a place, chances are good that another muley will find it soon after. So if you do find one, your best tactic is to return for another trophy buck.

Here are a few of my trophy bucks all taken from the same area.
(Courtesy of Cheri Flory.)

18

Hunting Downwind

I hate French restaurants. Usually, going to one means that I'll have to wear a tie, or at least a sports coat, apparel that I dislike wearing. I'm more at home in a Maine guide shirt and a pair of jeans. For that reason, hunting downwind suits me just fine. The dirtier my hunting clothes become, the better it works, so I can wear the same clothes all season and they become more and more useful the grimier they get. This makes for less laundry. Since I'm a bachelor these days, and I hate to do laundry, I usually bribe a lady friend to do my wash. Unfortunately, she loves French restaurants, and a trip to one is her price.

In addition to the obvious advantage of dirtying fewer clothes, using your own scent to drive game to your hunting companions or to a place where you can get a shot can be a pretty effective technique. Don't be concerned about dribbling bacon grease on your pants (unless you're in grizzly country!), standing in the smoke of a campfire, or letting your own juices soak into that new wool shirt. Your hunting buddies may refuse to get downwind of you, but the dirtier your clothes get, the more you can be sure that game can smell you.

Using your scent to drive game to companions is comparatively simple. It also has the advantage over conventional driving in that, if done correctly, there is seldom a need for more than one driver.

Scent Driving In Timber

High-elevation basins are common in much Western big-game country, and they are ideal places in which to employ "scent driving" (as I'll call it). In many basins, especially on the north and east exposures, there is timber and thick brush in the bottom or up to the throat of the basin. In such country, it's best to post "sitters" around the semicircle of the basin above the timber. Game will usually move out of the timber that's located along well-used trails, so sitters should wait near these trails. During the day, in most cases, the

128

air heats and becomes less dense so the breeze is uphill, into the faces of the sitters. Though deer can be moved with only one driver, more might be better with an exceptionally large stand of trees, and a single driver can improve his chances by hanging bits of clothing on bushes at the lower, upwind end of the timber.

Once, with four hunters already in place at the upper end of a basin, I left my grimy cowboy hat on a branch on the upwind side of the timber, tied a sweaty bandanna on another bush a few yards farther on, left my coat hanging from a pine a bit farther along, tied the horse to another pine, draped the saddle over a deadfall (sweaty side up), and finally, toward the edge of the timber stand, hung the saddle blanket. There was a strong breeze blowing up the canyon through my line of smelly objects, and into the timber. I took my time, since it would take awhile for my scent to disperse through the trees, before moving in myself. I moved across the wind, from one side of the stand to the other, and then back. I did this several times. When the shooting ended, two of the sitters had taken good bucks and a third had missed an elk. The fourth, Lem, had fallen asleep on a log.

This country hadn't been hunted too hard, so it wasn't difficult to move the bucks. In areas that receive heavy hunting pressure, bucks are apt to sit tighter, so it's necessary to move more slowly and make more passes through a given stand of timber or brush. The same strategy can work as well on flat ground, but in such a case, it's even more important to post sitters near the trails that lead from the stand of timber. It may also be better to use more sitters, since they won't be able to see as far as those who are posted on hills or slopes.

Pushing game with scent when you're alone is a bit more of a trick, one that's easier to pull off when you're pushing smaller stands of timber. Move slowly across the upwind side of the stand, giving your scent time to permeate the brush, and leave articles of clothing (if practical) as you go. If you need to relieve yourself, this is a good place to do it. Then, circle as quietly and quickly as you can and get to the downwind side of the stand where you expect game to move from. The thing that makes this type of maneuver possible is that scent usually takes awhile to disperse into brush and it often takes animals some time before they decide to move, thus giving the solo hunter time to get downwind of the stand and intercept them. It's very important to move quietly to the downwind side of the stand. If game hears you crashing about, they'll know something's amiss and will not be predictably driven, and it's necessary to be able to predict where they will go if you're alone.

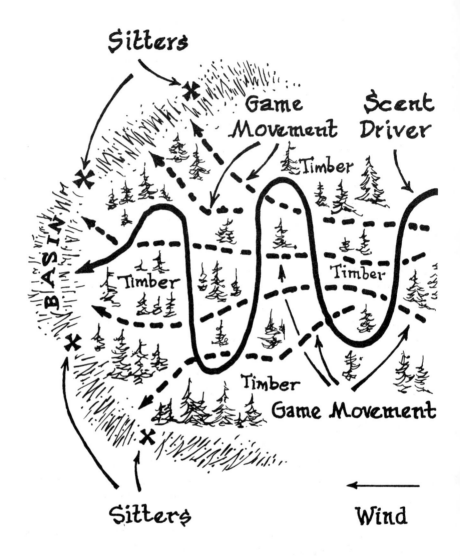

Scent driving in a timbered basin.

Scent Driving In Canyons

Canyons in the West are often timbered only in the bottoms, where there's water, or on the north- and east-facing slopes that receive less sunlight and lose less moisture to evaporation. In pushing canyons that only have timber or heavy brush in the bottom, post sitters along the sides of the canyon on the open slopes, and/or at the head of the canyon. If your supply of sitters is limited or the canyon is very large, have the sitters move along the slopes several hundred yards ahead of the driver in the bottom. Again, the wind is normally up-canyon during daylight hours when it is less dense. This might not always be the case—if it's blowing down-canyon for some reason, such as an approaching cold front, or across-canyon, simply put the driver where his scent will be carried to where the deer are likely to be—in this case, the canyon bottom. The driver simply moves downwind through the brush in the bottom, which may be anywhere from 10 to more than 100 yards wide (in the wider bottoms, grid across the brush so you don't miss any deer). Deer will generally move away from the driver, up-canyon if they're not badly frightened. Some may move up one of the side slopes where the sitters or even the driver might get a shot. In some canyon bottoms, the timber may be predominately conifers, evergreen trees and shrubs that are easy to walk through. In others there may be dense, nearly impenetrable tangles of willows, chokecherry, or aspen saplings. As a rule, to the driver's woe, the thicker the timber is, the more likely it is to hold game.

In canyons that are timbered on the north and east exposures, it may be wise to post sitters along game trails that lead into the timber, yet positioned so they can also shoot across the canyon to the open south- or west-facing slope. Another good place to post sitters is along the side canyons that radiate out from the main canyon. Game trails often lead up the bottoms of these side canyons.

Pushing a canyon by yourself is, again, a bit trickier than driving deer to other hunters. The solo hunter has to be quicker, usually quieter, and more alert. When driving up a canyon by yourself, move downwind through the brush in the canyon bottom for a while, then climb up onto one of the open slopes to check out the opposite slope. Next, move back down into the bottom and then up onto the opposite slope, keeping your eyes peeled for game. Be sure to pause long enough in the bottom to let the wind carry your scent up-canyon. Repeat the procedure as many times as necessary until you get to the head of the canyon. Keep especially alert at the head, since canyon heads often act as a sort of temporary dam, holding up game that have been moving up-canyon through the brush. Game, especially deer, dislike leaving a canyon that they are familiar with, even more so if it involves a dash across open terrain.

If the wind is drifting down the canyon for some reason, simply move from the head of the canyon toward its mouth. If the wind is drifting across the canyon, walk along the upwind side so that your scent will drift down into the timber or brush. In many ways, this is the best way to hunt with your scent, since you're in the open and can always see, and most game will move onto the open, opposite slope. Unfortunately, it also seems to be the rarest wind direction.

I've also found scent-driving to be effective while float-hunting for moose in the Arctic. Many of the rivers turn on themselves often, forming peninsulas of willow-choked beach where moose frequently feed and bed. It's no difficult trick to find peninsulas where the wind is blowing toward its tip. Having done this, all the hunter has to do is move quickly from the base of the peninsula toward its end on the river bend. He can usually get there as the moose is swimming across or as it climbs onto the beach on the other side. I've employed this tactic on other rivers for mule deer and I have a friend who uses a variation of it regularly for whitetails in Montana.

There are other situations in other types of terrain where scent driving will work, but the theory remains the same. The idea, always, is to put yourself in a position where the wind drifts your scent to where you suspect deer or other game are hiding, and then to position yourself or your companions where they can get a shot when game moves.

By the end of the season my hunting clothes can just about stand by themselves. With any kind of luck, I can go through two or three deer hunts, an elk or antelope hunt, and probably a float hunt for moose and caribou before I accumulate enough dirty clothes so I need to ask my lady friend to do the laundry, which means putting on a tie for a dinner at a French restaurant. But I'll admit that by then it's almost worth it.

19

Floating For River-Bottom Bucks

One of the many challenges of a mule deer hunt is finding a place with plenty of deer and very few hunters. As more and more sportsmen take up deer hunting in the West, this becomes harder to do; but there is one area that is frequently overlooked—the land along the rivers. River bottoms often get little hunting pressure, while the surrounding higher country is crawling with hunters. As a result, the deer are pushed into the bottom lands where they can hide, sometimes in incredible numbers. If the river is somewhat inaccessible, so much the better; the harder it is for hunters to get to, the more likely it is to hold deer.

The way to hunt this buck-rich country is to float it. Fortunately, no matter how different Western rivers may appear to be, the methods used to float them for mule deer are the same regardless of which body of water you choose.

Peninsulas

Rivers seldom run straight courses. They twist and turn on themselves, forming small peninsulas that are ideal places to drive deer, whether alone or with a companion or two. Of course, it's easier to drive with one or more companions. Then, the driver or drivers are let off at the base of the peninsula and the shooter floats downstream, banking the boat across the river from the peninsula tip. There, ideally, he'll be able to see both banks of the peninsula and spot any deer crossing the river. The driver works slowly across the base of the peninsula until he hits the river on the other side, then turns and repeats the maneuver, working gradually back and forth toward the peninsula tip. Generally, river-bottom brush is thick, so the grid made by drivers should be fine, especially if the hunting season has been open for a few days and immigrant bucks from the surrounding country are sitting tight.

If you're hunting alone, make one or two quick passes across the base of the peninsula and then move quickly and quietly toward its tip. Generally, there will be an initial rush of deer trying to clear the area, and if the solo

133

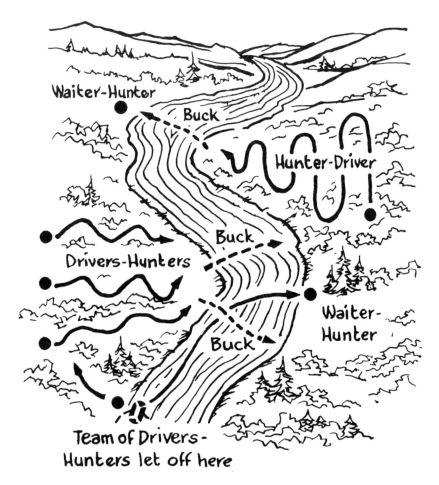

Driving or "pushing" river-bottom bucks to posted hunters.

hunter moves fast enough, he can get to the end of the peninsula as deer are crossing or climbing out on the other side. (I've used this method for moose in the Arctic, and have a friend who uses it regularly for whitetails in Montana.) Then, the lone hunter should work quietly up one bank, back toward the base of the peninsula again and make a quick pass or two across it—hopefully to start or unnerve any deer that are sitting tight. The hunter should then head for the river, moving as quietly as possible along the shore toward the peninsula tip, and wait in a place where he can watch both sides. Often, it takes a while for some deer to sneak out, and they'll do that more readily if they believe you're still near the base of the peninsula.

Canyons

Commonly, there are small canyons and ravines that are accessible only from the river. These are often hot places to find a good buck. Again, it's easier if you're working with one or more companions because that way at least one man can work up the often brushy ravine bottoms and another can sidehill, watching for bucks pushed out of the brush. If you're alone, work up the bottom slowly, climbing onto the ravine side frequently in order to watch the opposite slope, then repeat the procedure on the other side. Solo ravine or canyon hunting works best if you're moving downwind with the breeze carrying your scent up-canyon ahead of you. This is usually the case during the day when the air is warming, becoming less dense, and moving uphill.

Islands

Hunting islands is similar to hunting peninsulas but more fun, especially if the island is more than an acre or two in size and you have few, if any, drivers. It's more exciting because if you jump a buck, it has to cross water in order to escape the island, and even if you're alone, you can hear it splashing. Then you can rush toward the splash and be ready for a shot after the deer has climbed onto the opposite shore. (Don't shoot the animal while it is in the water; in some places, it's illegal, and it's certainly unsporting. Also, check regulations about the legality of shooting from a boat.)

On larger islands, blessedly not too plentiful in mule deer country, it helps to have more than one hunter, or even more than one driver. The drivers start at the upriver end of the island after the shooter has floated to the downriver end. The man on stand (the shooter) should position himself so he can see down both banks of the island, if possible. Drivers should make a wavery course toward the man on stand (one driver alone would make a grid back and forth across the island). Drivers should stay ready and listen for bucks splashing into the river. If the island is large or particularly thick and the drivers are few, it's wise to make more than one pass down the length of it.

Crossings And Watering Sites

Another good technique to try when float hunting for mule deer is to watch for crossing and watering places. If there is a concentration of tracks on one bank and another concentration on the opposite shore, the place is a crossing. I know of several such places—one on the Yellowstone north of Gardiner, another on the Wyoming Green, and a third on the Dolores River—where deer either leave the thick cover along the river or come down from rimrocks or hills to cross and feed in alfalfa or grass-hay fields. A place like that is a consistently good producer, and if you find such a hotspot, you may want to spend the entire season right there. It will probably be easy enough to collect a legal buck, but real trophies will still be hard to come by, as they always are. Most older bucks are nocturnal during hunting seasons, though from time to time they may be tempted out earlier in the evening, especially if it's been very hot and dry or there's a field of succulent alfalfa just across the river. The crossing will be used at night, very early in the morning (usually before sunup), and late in the evening, so waiting early and late in the day is the best tactic. You might want to look for a big track and follow it to the buck's bed, which should be located somewhere in the surrounding area. Tracking is often successful, since river-bottom bucks seldom stray far.

Ambushing at watering places, which are frequently where a canyon or ravine comes to the river or where a ledge or slope leads to high country, is also good and is best after a very hot day. Then, the techniques used are pretty similar to those used when ambushing at a crossing.

Early And Late Floating

Another method is to simply float early and late in the day. Mule deer feed more actively around dawn and dusk, so these are prime times to float. Bear in mind that it's difficult to shoot accurately from a boat that's rocking in the current, and in places it's actually against the law, so when you do see a buck you want, work your boat to shore as quietly as possible. Deer, like most other big game, don't seem to be frightened of objects floating in the current, at least not from a distance. Having watched the reactions of a number of animals to my approach in a raft or canoe, I firmly believe that they thought I was either some floating debris or a swimming animal. But when you're closer and they can pick out detail or smell you, they'll head for the brush.

One recent day, I'd just left Paradox Valley on the quickening current of the Dolores River as the November sun climbed above the looming rimrocks. The wind had been blustery and downriver all morning, and several times bucks had scented me and bounded away out of rifle range. I beached the canoe on a tiny sand island and lay down in the sun, trying to get the cold out of my bones and forget the frustration. In spite of the day's bad luck, I was glad that I hadn't seen another floater all season and had the river to myself, and I knew I'd get a buck eventually. Lulled by the familiar rush of the river and the wet smell of sand and river mud, I closed my eyes against the glare. I was startled awake by the towering red rimrocks—and a buck staring at me from across the river. Sometimes, the deer find you.

Float Facts

I've floated in dories, canoes, and inflatable rafts, and have come to prefer the last. They're quieter, dependable, tough, and forgiving (you can make a lot of mistakes before you get in trouble with one). They have the added advantage of being handy to transport, and when deflated, fit easily into the back of a station wagon. Good-quality inflatables include Achilles, Avon, and Riken.

Glass or wood canoes are fairly quiet if you're careful, but not as quiet as inflatables. They are also easier to turn over in rough water or if you're not paying attention. Aluminum canoes are just too noisy.

Dories are fine in the right hands on larger rivers, but they are too noisy and awkward for my tastes, and it's difficult to get them in and out of rivers without a boat ramp.

Many Western streams can be low during autumn hunting seasons, so draft can be a consideration. Rafts and canoes can carry a surprising amount of weight and still maintain a shallow draft.

There are scores of rivers that are suitable for float hunting for mule deer. Those I've experienced include the Green (both in Wyoming and Utah), the Dolores and San Miguel in Colorado, and the Yellowstone in Montana. There are probably twenty more in Montana, a number of them in Idaho (including the Salmon and Snake), and smaller streams in eastern Wyoming, Colorado, and Utah.

In many places in the West, river bottoms are private property. As yet, at least in much of Colorado and Montana, few areas are posted, but it may be a good idea to get permission, anyway. In some places, it's the law.

Cheri Flory floating for river-bottom bucks.

20

Home On The Range

Most buck hunters spend the majority of their hunting time where there are no big bucks. Actually, throughout most of the season, trophy mule deer bucks live in a very small area, and these areas, called the home range, are not around four-wheel-drive roads or places accessible to ATV's. All a hunter has to do, really, to locate a big buck's home range, is to find big tracks (the forehoof of an adult buck is 3½-4 inches long), scrapes, and rubs (mule deer scrape and rub for completely different reasons than do whitetails). Then, to maximize his valuable time afield, a hunter confines his efforts to this home range.

Home Range

A big muley buck spends 90% of his time in a small area. Unlike whitetails, mule deer bucks may have as many as half a dozen home ranges as they migrate up from winter range at, say, 4,000 feet in late spring, to late-summer/autumn range at 9,000 feet in early autumn. More typically, most bucks have perhaps four home ranges in a given year, depending on the buck and the terrain. Fall home ranges I've measured over the years varied from 1/8th square mile to over a mile-and-a-half in diameter, depending mostly on cover and feed availability.

It's my theory that a given buck uses the same home ranges year after year as he climbs to summer range, and then descends again late in the fall. I do know that certain bucks show up in the same place each year on their late summer/early autumn range. One example was a buck I traced during the 70's. He appeared on the same small slope each opening-day eve. He fed there, then walked around the slope and bedded in a dense tangle of Douglas fir, blue spruce, big-toothed maple, and chokecherry. I noticed him first when he was 2½ years-old. He was a tiny 4 x 5 then, with one abnormal "cheater" point sticking an inch out of the main beam of his right antler. He was back again the following season, with the same number of points and that cheater

139

tine in exactly the same place; his antlers were higher, a bit wider, and he was bigger through the body, weighing around 150 lbs. on the hoof. He was a good piece of meat, but no trophy, so I didn't even think of collecting him. He was back again the next season, and the one after. That year he was bigger and rounded through the haunches and shoulders; his antlers were heavier, wider and higher, and that cheater tine was about four inches long; he was 4½ years old that season, and almost a trophy buck. I had a hard time not shooting him. The only time I saw him that season was on the eve of the opening, and once again in the predawn half-light as he disappeared into the tangle where he spent the day. Even though I'd never hunted him, he'd learned to keep low and to the timber during hunting season. I'd decided to try and collect him that next season. He'd be 5½ then and a good trophy. The only problem was that he didn't show up on that slope where he fed, though his big tracks were there. He'd become totally nocturnal where feeding in the open was concerned. I stillhunted slowly into the tangle of brush and timber, trying to stalk silently along a well-used game trail, noting his big, outward pointing tracks. Before long, I found a rub on a fir sapling, then several more on four-inch diameter willows. There were several fresh beds scattered through the trees, each four-feet long, fresh tracks, and soft and pliable droppings. This was where the buck lived. I backed slowly out of the tangle, hoping fervently I hadn't frightened him, then climbed onto the ridge, well away from the place, and sat on a boulder to think it over. I knew he was there, even though I hadn't seen him.

Alright, I told myself, *he's not coming out, so you've got to go in after him.* I already knew a little of what the interior of that hair-thick tangle looked like: I knew where the seep was, where he'd bedded in the recent past, where he vented his increasing aggression on saplings as the rut approached, and I knew the main trail to and from the feeding slope. I knew about him and at least some of his routines. If I was lucky, he didn't know I was plotting to get him, and therein lay my advantage.

In the dawn, I eased to the rim of the ravine and looked in. The buck wasn't feeding on his slope, but that was no surprise, since I didn't really expect him to be. His big tracks were there as he meandered and browsed. I worked down the same trail into the center of his home range, noting that his big tracks were imprinted deeply over the ones I'd made the day before; I hadn't frightened him away after all. Then I was stalking through the collection of beds and rubbed saplings, and one had been worked over recently. Strips of bark hung from the willow. I eased into thicker trees and then suddenly, he was there, nibbling at fungi growing from a rotted blowdown. He turned quickly to stare as I brought up the .270, and the shot killed him as he bunched his muscles to jump. The buck in his five plus years had never been disturbed in that tangle, had no reason to believe he would be, and let his guard down. That's the advantage of sneaking into a mule buck's "center area." (Some whitetail, as well as muley, writers and biologists use the term "core area," but since that term has been used to define a number of different concepts, I'll use "center area," a term I coined in the early 70's while researching deer behavior as a biologist.)

Most bucks don't expect trouble in their center area. On the other hand, shooting is apt to be quick and close and you'll only get one shot, so you've got to be as ready as a grouse hunter approaching a point. The center area is typically in thick brush or timber, so moving quietly through it can be a bit of a trick. Think *slow and quiet*. Wear wool or other "quiet" clothing and soft-soled footgear such as moccasins or sneakers.

Scouting

Most preseason scouting relies on sighting bucks. Actually, scouting for the home range is a better way to find trophy bucks because you don't have to rely on sighting, and since most sightings are made after the buck has already sighted you, you're less likely to frighten the buck out of the country. To locate a buck's home range, look instead for tracks and trails, rubs, beds, droppings, escape cover, browse plants, and even scrapes (these don't have the same significance of whitetail scrapes).

Each buck's trail is different: some are so fat their tracks point outward at an exaggerated angle; some have tell-tale hoof chips or scars; others may limp slightly from an old injury. Find a big track, identify it, then look for it in the surrounding countryside. Where you see that track is the buck's home range, so confine your hunting there. There may be a heavy concentration of tracks on the open slope across the gully; that's where the buck feeds, and hunting him there is best very late just before dark and early in the dawn.

Chances are, though, that a trophy buck will be nocturnal, so laying an ambush at a feeding area may not work. For confirmation, look for freshly cropped shrubs. The cut of freshly nibbled twigs is light and moist; older cuts are brown, more oxidized and dry. There will likely be a well-used trail from that slope to heavy brush somewhere nearby. The buck uses the trail to go between the feeding and center areas. Follow the trail carefully into the timber, as I did. In autumn, there will be some barked saplings where the buck polished his antlers and relieved some of his increasing aggression and libido. Larger bucks generally rub larger saplings—usually around 4-inches in diameter; small bucks almost always used smaller saplings. If you're out scouting and find such a place, back slowly away, especially if all this sign is fresh. You don't want to frighten the buck and send him over the divide, or even make him more wary before hunting season.

Rubs and beds close together usually indicate you're in a buck's "center area." If you're scouting thoroughly, you'll find older and dryer rubs some distance away from the center area. These are where that or other bucks shed velvet and polished antlers earlier in the season. Those in the center area will be fresher, at least if the buck is still using it, some so fresh sap might be oozing from wounds.

While scouting some years back, I blundered right through what I came to recognize later as the center area of a buck's home range. There were half a dozen thoroughly barked saplings around a small seep, and sap was oozing out of several, indicating their freshness. There were three or four beds within a few yards of the rubs, mostly under fir trees. Fortunately, the buck was out at the time or I'd have scared him into Wyoming. Even though I didn't know at the time that I was in the buck's center area, I did understand that there was an awful lot of fresh "sign" around. I came back the following week when the hunt opened, seated myself across the ravine in the pre-dawn darkness, and waited for daylight. It came, I waited. The sun was high when I noticed the swaying of a big willow. Other trees weren't moving, there was no wind, so I knew the buck was at it again. I eased silently down the ridge to a place where I could see into the tangle. The buck was hidden in brush. Finally, wearied of battering that sapling, he stepped into a small opening and began pawing a bed. The shot was anticlimactic, and the buck was a good one.

By October, bucks rub more and more vigorously. You'll see most rubs where a buck spends most of his time, in the center and feeding areas, so these are the places to look for trophies. But unless the weather is unseasonably cold and snowy or the hunting pressure light, don't waste much time on the feeding area since a wise old buck will probably only be there at night. Concentrate on rubs near beds, either by stillhunting in the center area, or by waiting along the main trail near rubs.

Veteran bucks bed in thick timber or brush, usually near canyon heads or ridge tops where they can slip into the next drainage if frightened by a hunter. As with any lesson that really stays with you, I learned this one the hard way.

I'd been hunting up a long ravine, hoping to find a big buck I'd seen on the opening. I was still 400 yards away from a thick growth of maples at the ravine head when two bucks burst through it, raced across the open saddle, and disappeared into the next drainage. They never paused to look back, even though they were out of rifle range. Both were big, but the leading buck was the one I'd seen earlier and so big there could be no mistaking him for another. I was sick about it; even as that huge, wide-spreading rack disappeared over the ridge I knew I should have stillhunted that buck's center area at the canyon head first, and not from below.

That was a dumb mistake, and it cost me. And I've made others—sometimes I'm a slow learner. But because of such blunders, I've learned. These days, I have a good idea where a buck will bed once I've found his home range. It's usually near a canyon head in thick brush or timber. I've learned you don't frighten a buck from below. If you're in timber, you don't frighten him at all, so you watch wind direction, you scan carefully ahead and to the sides, and you stalk as silently as a snake.

Tactics

If you've got a companion, stationing him above the center area if it's not so large a buck just loses himself in it, and then driving from below is good tactic. I've teamed up with friends and collected a few bucks this way. Probably, though, the center area will be located in a large stand of timber and if you frighten a buck there, he just retreats farther into the trees without ever crossing the open. Tracking and stillhunting here are the only alternatives, but then that's the best way to stalk anyway. There's a very good feeling when you track a buck to his bed and kill him at forty feet as he chews his cud. When you can do that, you'll feel proud, and you have every right to be.

Another alternative is to ambush the buck along the trail he uses to and from feeding areas. Normally, a big buck is smart enough to be more or less nocturnal during hunting season. But once in a while he'll slip and stay out feeding a bit late in the morning, or come out early in the evening, especially if there's been light hunting pressure. If you're not pressed for time, wait early and late at the trail between the center and the feeding areas. I've taken several bucks this way.

Feed Plants

Another thing to look for, when hunting a buck's home range, is feed plants. Typically, bucks feed on a variety of forbs, grass seed-heads, and shrubs. It's not necessary to know what they're called—the deer don't—but it is important to be able to recognize them in the field. Since in any area bucks will feed on the same things as does and small bucks, it's a good idea to watch what smaller deer are eating so you don't frighten the big buck. Note what they're eating. It might be wise to make sketches of the plants so you don't have to repeat the field work a few years down the line.

At times, it helps to age browsed plants. Three seasons ago, I'd found the home range of a good buck two weeks before the opener. It was in a steep, short ravine that had all the right things—plenty of feed, water, escape cover, and a dense tangle of scrub oak and aspens for the center area. The tracks were big, the rubs on saplings to seven inches in diameter, and there were plenty of cropped shrubs (wild rose, bitterbrush, curlleaf mahogany, forbs) on the slope where he'd been feeding. I thought I had it in the bag. But when I checked the cuts where the shoots had been nipped off a day before the opening, they were brown, oxidized and old. The buck for some reason had left. Perhaps he'd been frightened off by elk hunters, since that hunt had ended four days earlier.

Later that season, I found another buck's home range by glassing for deer browse. In northern Utah, western Wyoming, and parts of Colorado, Arizona and Nevada, deer have a decided preference for a belly-high, shiny-leaved shrub called by locals chaparral and by others manzanita. Aside from coniferous trees, it's the only thing still green during autumn hunting seasons, and it can be located at great distances. I was sitting on the ridge that afternoon, noting where there were extensive stands of it as far away as four miles. If the stands were well away from 4-wheel-drive tracks, they had possibilities. Furthermore, if they were near larger stands of timber or heavy brush for cover, so much the better. If it seemed water might be nearby, though that wasn't critical, all the better. I found one place that seemed through the spotting scope to be ideal.

The next morning, I hiked down into the canyon, then over a ridge, into another ravine, over another ridge, and so on, until I reached the canyon. I set up camp on the opposite ridge so as not to disturb a buck, if there was one. There were all sorts of deer tracks and freshly cropped shrubs. Across the canyon was a dense stand of timber, an ideal bedding area, and farther down the creek was more timber and heavy stands of oaks and maples. I wandered around for awhile before I finally found a big deer track. I back-trailed the track, and it led down a well-trod path towards a stand of timber. I'd already suspected the place to be the center area for a big buck if there was one around, so I tried to decide what to do. Darkness was coming rapidly, and if I made a stalk into the timber, I'd have to hurry it. I decided to leave the buck where he was and try again when my odds were better.

After several days of stillhunting and familiarizing myself with the place, I caught a glimpse of the buck. He was just disappearing into the timber as darkness faded. The light was poor, but it was easy to see he was huge. I tried waiting along the trail between the bedding and center area for several days without luck. Finally, I decided to stillhunt into the buck's center area to see if he was home. Actually, I was pretty sure he would be, but I'd have to move slowly and carefully if I were to get a shot, and even if I did, it would have to be taken on an instant. The odds were in favor of the buck, which is why big mulies live in such tangles in the first place. The breeze was drifting slowly downhill in the cold, dense air as I eased along the trail toward the center area, straining to see as far into the dawn gloom of the trees as possible. I knew that before long the wind would change as the day warmed, and with the way the trail was heading, the buck would catch my scent. I had to move quickly. I found a rub a hundred yards into the timber, and then another, and another. I looked around carefully, straining to find a piece of the buck. I noticed an old bed beneath a spruce. My palms were sweating, in spite of sub-freezing temperatures. I took a step, looked around, took another, and watched and listened. Out of the corner of my eye, I caught a movement down the slope. A spruce sapling jerked forward and back, and then I saw the buck's antlers as he horned it again. I was in the buck's line of vision, but since he'd always been secure in this stand of timber and he was busy beating up on a sapling, he'd missed seeing me. When he hooked the spruce again, I brought the rifle up. He'd sensed something and looked up. The .270 roared in the silent timber and the bullet hit the buck in the base of the neck as he stood facing me.

Not infrequently, a big buck may abandon his home range on opening day for safer and more remote haunts. But often, the buck will return in a few days when things quiet down again. I'd done my homework one year, and had found a good buck's home range. I thought I knew it so intimately that I could predict where the buck would be at any given time of day. I'd checked on the buck each weekend for over a month and he seemed very secure. Then came opening morning, and he was gone. It was hard for me to believe he'd left, so hard, in fact, that I hunted the place for several days before I could accept his departure. I gave up and hunted elsewhere.

In Utah, where I've competed with tens of thousands of buck hunters for too many years, most hunting occurs on opening weekend. After that, the pressure eases, and apparently the buck noticed the same thing, because when I checked on the next to the last day of the season, the buck was back. I didn't get him that day, but I did the next by stillhunting very slowly into his center area and killing him in his bed.

Don't waste valuable time wandering randomly around the mountains. Instead, locate by tracks and other "sign" a trophy buck's home range, and stay in this relatively small area. You may have to hunt more carefully and quietly than you've ever had to before, but if you do, you can stalk into a buck's center area and perhaps even kill him in his bed. When you can do that, you've probably just done the hardest thing in North American hunting today, and that will be cause enough for a celebration.

Where the deer and the antelope play.

21

Stalking Alpine Muleys

Early, high-country hunting seasons in relatively wild country are a good bet for the trophy hunter in good physical condition. In addition, backpack hunters into the wilderness can get away from other hunters, since significantly fewer redshirts are going to expend the effort to climb to remote, timberline basins.

Since fewer, if any, other hunters are getting into remote high country, trophy bucks are less cautious, and easier to bag. In heavily hunted lower country, big bucks are nocturnal for the most part; up high, it's not uncommon to find a big buck out browsing in the daylight in the early morning or late afternoon and evening. Then, planning a stalk and carrying it out is easier because bucks tend to be less wary.

Basin Bucks

Frequently, adult bucks bed in open basins, and watch below, since this is the logical approach for a predator, whether it's a mountain lion or a redshirt with a .270. During the day the air is typically warming and drifting up the slope, carrying scent to the buck, even if the old boy misses seeing danger below, which is unlikely given the muley's extraordinary vision. I'd never attempt stalking from below unless there was absolutely no other alternative. It's the buck stalker's good fortune that high country is also rough country, and usually offers plenty of stalking cover. Since it's imperative not to give your scent to the buck, you've got to stalk the buck either from above or more or less the same altitude. Here, use rocks, ridges, or ravines as cover. Stalking from above often seems the only approach; then the wind is in your face carrying scent *and* small sounds away from the buck, and the buck is almost invariably facing downhill, away from you. Bucks in steep and rocky terrain hear rocks rolling all the time, so pay little attention to small noises you might make, however if you make them regularly, a buck is going to get curious and check you out. If you're cautious and pay attention to all details, stalking from above is a good tactic. But if you're not especially careful stalking from above, it's too easy to make small mistakes which will tip you off to the buck. I've killed good bucks in the Ruby Mountains of Nevada, the country east of Afton, Wyoming, and in the Wellsville Mountains (the steepest range in the United States) in northern Utah by stalking from above.

Timber Bucks

Alpine bucks also bed in the timber that is frequently found at the lower end or throat of high basins. Typically they feed out of the trees early and late, then bed down during the day in the timber. Here, employ the methods discussed in the chapter "Muleys in Timber" and other chapters, that is, track and stillhunt slowly. Since alpine bucks tend to be less cautious than their lowland cousins, they may not always bed downwind of their backtrail, so straight tracking (as opposed to using the loop or parallel methods) often works; it's also less time-consuming and difficult.

If you've got a few days, and you're fairly sure the buck is feeding into the open early and late, set an ambush. Get as far away from where the buck feeds out of the timber so there's little possibility of his getting your scent, since mountain winds are unpredictable, or hearing you, and still feel good about your ability to hit him.

Ambushing is a pleasant way to hunt unless it's too cold; then, it's miserable. If the weather is warm, you can stare out across sizable chunks of spectacular alpine scenery, read a book, and meditate. If it's cold, I won't sit still long, so I'll stillhunt or track down into the trees.

Another advantage of hunting in mountain range-top basins and along ridges is that you're closer to heaven than down in the lowlands.

Me with a good buck taken in the high country.
I'm the one with the beard, by the way.

22

Stories In Snow

About December my blood thickens, slows, and if I'm not careful, I slip into a kind of pre-hibernation lethargy. Physicians and psychiatrists have Latin names for this, but hunters know the real reason: the latest hunts have ended and the next ones are nine interminable months off. Most of us substitute something in hunting's place—reloading, fondling guns, gazing wistfully at old trophies. Many of us must also get out, in spite of single-digit temperatures and blizzards that can dump two feet in a few hours. I don boot-pacs, gaitors, longjohns, wool, mittens, down and pile, grab snowshoes or cross-country skis, binoculars and thermos, and wander out onto winter range. Over the years, these off-season "hunts" have become as important as earlier ones where I actually carry a rifle, not only because they relieve cabin fever, but because I learn and practice.

Sheepherd Canyon, Utah, Late December

Four inches of new, powdery snow make excellent tracking conditions, and the squall had just raced off toward Colorado. The feeble sun eased into the sub-zero, newly-frosted canyon, and mule deer browsed hectically to make up for time lost sitting out the storm. I still-hunted along the creek (even though I didn't carry a gun), stopping occasionally to glass for good bucks, before cutting a big track that came off a timbered slope and meandered onto a bare ridge. I measured the fore-print with a .270 cartridge I carried for just that purpose (it's exactly 3¼ inches long), and the track is a half-inch longer, so it belongs to a *good* muley (the largest foretrack I've ever measured went 4¼, but big bucks more typically range from 3½ to 4-inches in length). The big track was just what I'd come for, too, because I wanted to track down and ritually "bag" a trophy buck.

The buck was walking (his stride averaged 23-inches on the flat and slightly shorter when climbing, and the hindhoof was placed almost precisely in the print left by the forehoof), so he's at ease. From time-to-time he'd break into

151

a trot (the stride here is between 33 and 38-inches, and the prints are slightly splayed), but he's still at ease. Mule deer trot almost as often as they walk. Deer are less apt to make mistakes when walking or trotting than when hurrying, because they have more time and concentration to sense danger. That's one reason the biggest bucks seldom run; they know they're more visible and more likely to miss important clues. The buck meandered through chaparral, bitterbrush and mountain mahogany, mule deer staples, and from the quantity of bark, twigs and small, shiny mahogany leaves on the snow, he was ravenous. The snow had quit shortly before dawn, so he'd browsed in daylight, something unheard of (except during the rut) during hunting seasons. Then, adult bucks are almost exclusively nocturnal.

The trail led across an open slope as the buck browsed and meandered from bush to bush, before leading up a shallow ravine toward the ridge above. Before long, it began to meander again, but this time he wasn't feeding; he was looking for a bed. Judging from the trail, he'd select it just as carefully as he would during hunting season. He wandered out to a point, stood a moment as if contemplating its bedding potential, then decided against it and climbed farther up the ridge. I trailed cautiously, watching above, aware the air was warming and rising and the buck would eventually scent any danger below, even if he didn't see it. A sixth sense told me he'd already bedded, and a moment later I was somehow convinced of it. I could almost "feel" his stare, but he at least hadn't scented anything or he'd have raced off. I carefully scanned above with binoculars; it took several minutes to locate the heavy, teak antlers, and he *was* staring. My snow-camo had confused him, but a second later he stiffened with sudden realization as he caught human scent. He's a tough target bouncing in that stiff-legged bound that eats up rough terrain in a hurry. Probably I could have hit him as I swung ahead with an imaginary Model 700, but I couldn't be sure. I'd be cheating if I scored him as a collected trophy, so I followed farther.

He bounded across the slope for nearly fifty yards (clearing from 23 to 29 feet per bound, and the hind hooves print ahead of the forehooves and the left side slightly ahead of the right) before dropping into a less-tiring gallop. Bucks won't bound long—it requires too much energy—so when hunting, wait for a bounding buck to drop into a slower stride where he's easier to hit. He'd galloped into the timber, then stopped abruptly to watch his backtrail from the safety of trees, which is typical big-buck behavior; they seldom pause in the open, contrary to mythology. (Of course the buck had been long gone by the time I "read" this from the trail.) He trotted farther into a big stand of fir and spruce, and by early afternoon he'd begun to circle and meander again as he searched for a bed.

As I deciphered the hours-old trail, I was fairly certain he'd already bedded and was perhaps even watching me at that moment, so I made loops on the downwind side of the trail, returning to the track every fifty yards to be sure I was going in the right direction. When I'm "looping," I'm seldom in a place where a buck can scent me, even when he beds on the downwind side of his backtrail as adult mule deer bucks almost always do. I was squatting to examine droppings when I spotted antlers twenty yards off beneath boughs of a big fir. He hadn't scented me, since I was downwind, and he stared away at his backtrail. *Ease down on your fanny, boy,* I told myself, and felt the adrenalin kick in. I watched for several minutes, then badly imitated the alarm "chr-r-r-r" of a red squirrel (in spite of diligent practicing, I've never mastered this very useful call), and the buck stood, offering a perfect broadside so close even a one-eyed bat could hit him. He was mine, and in my fantasy I stood over him motionless in the snow and fondled those heavy antlers. I'd already "bagged" him, so I just watched as he stamped a forefoot in frustration and stared at his backtrail; he knew something was wrong, but he didn't know quite what. Finally, I stood, and he bolted, but I'd done what I'd set out to do, and he was the best one I'd "bagged" in half a dozen winters.

Owl Creek, Wyoming (January)

I eased through the cottonwoods and willows of the Owl Creek bottoms in four tracking-perfect inches of cold, dry snow. Muleys browsed on open alfalfa fields and low sagebrush hills as I searched for whitetails. Occasional whitetail does and small bucks jumped from the bottom-thickets, and muleys were in the bottoms, too—they go everywhere. Whitetails kept to thick cover. A decent 4 x 4 whitetail buck broke from a willow tangle and raced across an opening, and a moment later a muley did the same giving me a rare opportunity to compare mule and whitetail tracks and strides side-by-side. From body configuration and size, and antlers, I *guessed* the bucks at three-and-a-half or four-and-a-half years old (with enough experience correlating body size and antlers with annual dentition rings, you can make good guesses at a live buck's age). The whitetail's foretrack was a bit smaller than the muley's and more pointed at the tip, because he lives in forested bottoms where the soil is less rocky and not as apt to wear down hooves. Strides are normally a bit shorter than a muley's, too. Parallel and fifteen yards to the side, the muley bounced in that unique, characteristic stiff-legged bound, and I realized what I'd forgotten: whitetails have three basic strides—the gallop, trot and walk, and they're similar to a mule deer's. Muleys have four strides—the basic three plus that stiff-legged bound.

The whitetail galloped through stands of immense cottonwoods and dense willow tangles, then slowed to a trot, occasionally stopping to watch his backtrail. Again, I'd read this from "sign," since the buck had passed much earlier. He'd retreated upwind and couldn't scent me, so relied on sight. Once, he circled to get behind but the band of river-bottom brush was too narrow to do it without showing himself, so he continued up Owl Creek. I sat against a cottonwood in the sun and waited to give him time to calm. An hour later I took up the trail again, and he was walking, but still pausing to watch his backtrail, and he often was doing it in the open, something a mature muley buck in hunted country almost never does. Eventually, the trail began to meander with no evidence of browsing, so he was ready to bed. I "looped" downwind of the trail, even though the wind quartered into my face, just in case he'd somehow made an exaggerated buttonhook and gotten downwind. I stepped gingerly across creek ice, climbed a low cut bank, and found where the tracks disappeared into a very thick bramble tangle. Unexpectedly, he crashed straight at me at twenty-five yards, branches popping and flying like straw, and for a moment I was certain he'd turned the tables. Once out of the tangle, however, he raced off as I threw up an imaginary Model 94 and stuck one through his lights as twenty yards. I'd "collected" him, too.

While winter stalking isn't *quite* the same as hunting with a gun, it's a close second, and often it's the best you can do during the off-season. Perhaps because you're not carrying a gun and not so goal-oriented, you'll learn more about game behavior, tracking, stillhunting and stalking than you ever will when you're out to acquire a trophy or meat. You might consider winter range to be the graduate school of big-game hunting, where you'll learn all you need to become more successful in the "real world" of autumn hunting seasons. And maybe more important, consider it also a way to survive northern winters and acute cabin fever.

23

The Mule Deer Gun

"Get a .270"

When I asked *Field & Stream* executive editor and gun writer Dave Petzal for input on this chapter, his advice was, "Get a .270." Period. According to Dave, that could serve as the entire chapter. Legendary *Outdoor Life* shooting editor Jack O'Connor came to the same conclusion decades earlier. The .270 was his favorite cartridge, not only for mule deer, but nearly anything else. Warren Page, O'Connor's contemporary at *Field & Stream,* after testing everything from the .220 Swift to the .458 Winchester, reluctantly concluded that the .270 was the ultimate deer cartridge. I say reluctantly, because Page didn't want to agree with that "skinny, long-legged @#$%‡§ across the street" (Petzal's paraphrase of Page's comment about O'Connor at *Outdoor Life*).

Just as Page was Dave Petzal's hero, Jack O'Connor was mine. As an impressionable youngster reading O'Connor in the early 60s, what he said was biblical. I vowed to someday own a .270. After a number of detours, where I shot with the .303 Enfield, .30/06, 7mm Remington magnum and a few other cartridges, I did finally get that .270. It was a pre-1964 Winchester Model 70, O'Connor's favorite, and I customized it with a Fajen fiddle-back maple stock, added rosewood forend and grip ends and a Redfield 3-9x variable scope. I used the gun for years. Later, I bought a Remington Model 700 in .270, a lighter rig, though not by much, that no longer put the fingers on my hand to sleep if I carried it hung from a shoulder all day. I shot more game with the model 700 than with all the rifles that came after, or all those before. The .270 is a versatile and lethal gun in the right hands. I have since given my well-travelled model 700 to a bighorn sheep guide in Canada, and Cheri, my better half, now shoots the Model 70; she's refinished the stock and cut it down to fit her.

I bagged my first big mule deer with a "sporterized" .303 Enfield, a chopped down British military rifle. My dad bought the thing in an army surplus store, for, if memory serves, $30. Though I was no giant, the butt section of the two-part stock was much too short. Nevertheless, Dad and I jumped a huge buck on the mountain overlooking our house in northern Utah back in 1962, and I nailed the buck with the primitive iron sights on the second shot (the first one went wild, mostly due to buck fever). The gun fit so badly that it bloodied my lip. The buck, by the way, was one of the heaviest I ever killed, field dressing at 268 pounds.

That Christmas I got a "sporterized" .30/06 Springfield. I was ecstatic, and trudged through snow all winter to the orchard across the street and practiced with cheap, military ammo. The barrel had pretty well had it by the time I got the gun, and it was doing well to shoot under a 5-inch group at a hundred yards. I did shoot a small buck that autumn with it, though it may have been luck. Later, I traded the gun to my brother for something or other. That summer I saved up and bought a cheap but new FN Mauser in 7mm Remington magnum. I learned reloading from a neighbor and worked up a load using the 139 grain Hornady that would average 3/4 of an inch at a hundred yards. I had the barrel glass bedded which helped, too. I used the 7 mag for years, and had good results with it on antelope, deer, elk and two mountain goats. Finally, the bolt cracked and I got rid of the gun.

I then purchased and customized that Model 70 .270, and shot deer, antelope, elk and moose with it. The gun was too heavy, and toting it around mule deer mountains for a week at a time could compress three vertebrae. Then to the model 700 with a Redfield variable; the gun was lighter, but not by enough to make any real difference. Just the same, I shot the rig for over 20 years and killed more with it than all the guns I've used before or since. I've taken the model 700 .270 to Africa twice, have used it on eland, zebra, kudu, sable, wildebeeste, waterbuck, leopard, as well as the smaller antelope such as reedbuck, bushbuck, impala, lechwe and gazelles. In North America, that gun has killed nearly all of the continent's big game, including grizzly and one-ton Alaskan moose. The lesson here seems to be that the .270 *is* the best deer cartridge, if not the best all-around cartridge, period. Petzal, O'Connor and Page are right.

Since I gave away my favorite .270 to Ken Olynyk, a British Columbia bighorn sheep guide, for the outstanding job he did on my hunt with him, I have since made the Remington Model Seven in 7mm/08 my main gun. I'd traded for it a few years earlier, but had only used it on backpack sheep hunts, because it was so light and handy. I scoped the gun with a compact Leupold 2x-7x variable, had the trigger adjusted to remove the creep and get the pull down to about 2 pounds, and refitted the stock. The gun is short, light, handy, and I can carry it on wilderness backpack hunts with a minimum of effort. It's a joy to use, too, now that I'm getting used to the short, light barrel. With both of the .270s I had before, there was a lot of weight out front with the long barrels, and I used this weight to steady the sight picture when aiming. With the suddenly light barrel in the Model Seven, I had a tendency to overcompensate, expecting the long barrel and weight of the earlier guns, and then I had to concentrate to get the sight picture back down. Where I had only a second or two to make a shot, I had difficulties. One winter, however, I went out into the desert and practiced on jackrabbits, running and sitting. It was a bumper year for jacks, and I got lots of practice. Eventually, I got used to the light barrel and short gun, and I did get good on running jacks. My last time out I shot over 40% on running hares, and the shots ranged from 60 to 200 yards, with the average shot very near the 100-yard mark; that day, I fired nearly a hundred rounds in the 7mm/08. The practice apparently paid off; in the past two seasons, I bagged a bighorn, antelope, whitetail and five mule deer with nine shots.

I won't go into the stats of either the .270 or 7mm/08, except to say they're very similar. In fact, there's so little difference in numbers that no hunter or deer will be able to tell the difference in performance with similar bullet weights. In any case, enough has been said in any number of shooting articles and books by men more knowledgeable than I on the subject, Dave Petzal for example, that I feel it's redundant to talk statistics here. This book is about hunting, not shooting, and I speak of calibers, cartridges, and guns only as they relate to mule-deer hunting. I've yet to see a hunter or deer carrying around a chronograph.

I don't reload anymore, don't seem to have the patience for it, so I settle for the best performance I can find in factory ammo. The only factory ammo I've used in the 7mm/08 is the Remington 140-grain pointed soft point. I've gotten good penetration with the load, better than Remington's .270 150-grain core lokt, which is designed for penetration but which I've found occasionally breaks up if it hits bone. I've had that particular bullet break up badly on small animals as bushbuck and impala, but sometimes hold together surprisingly well on such big ones as sable, elk and kudu. In my experience, the core lokt is inconsistent. The 140-grain soft point in 7mm/08, on the other hand, presumably designed for light animals with thin skins, seems to work well penetrating big animals. The bullet went completely through a 500-pound bear, though it only hit rib bones, and completely through a big caribou. It typically gives excellent performance on deer-sized animals, again noticeably better than the .270, 150-grain core lokt. I've had good luck with Federal loads in the .270, by the way. Since the Remington 140-grain load works so well in my gun and under the conditions I hunt under, I haven't found the need to experiment with other loads for the 7mm/08.

Over the years, I've gotten good results with other calibers, including the .280, 7mm Mauser, and .264 magnum, and the .30/06. The .264 mag, like the 7mm mag mentioned earlier, is a little more than is needed for mule deer, and many hunters dislike the recoil. I've got a friend that swears by the .280, and I've had good luck with the cartridge what little I've shot with it. It doesn't shoot quite as flat as either the .270 or 7mm/08, however, and that can be a consideration in much of the mule deer's wide-open range. These days, I consider it more of a thrill and more skillful to stalk close enough for a short range shot, so I hate to admit that in the old days when I lacked the skill and knowledge to make such a stalk, a flat trajectory was a major consideration. I'd often shoot bucks across canyons at over 400 yards, and barroom stories to the contrary, that is an *extremely* long shot. Now, it seems much of my mule deer shooting is under 200 yards, so flat trajectory isn't that important. But it's best to be prepared for the rare long shot.

If you're trying to decide what cartridge to buy for mule deer, take Petzal's advice, get a .270. You can't go wrong, and the early gurus of gun writing, O'Connor and Page, felt the same. Actually, anything around the .270, the 7mm/08 especially, such as the 7mm Mauser, .280 or .284 Winchester, or the .30/06 make excellent mule deer guns. I wouldn't use anything smaller than 7mm on mule deer, however, since big bucks are tough and shooting conditions sometimes difficult, and a 100-grain .243 or 120-grain 6.5mm magnum bullet just won't kill a buck cleanly except under ideal conditions, and those are rare, given the trophy buck's cagey nature. My advice: either the lightweight Remington Model Seven 7mm/08 (I'm still pretty enthused with this gun!) or lightweight .270. Don't hunt with a gun straight off the rack; have a gunsmith fine-tune it. In my Model Seven, I had one get the trigger creep out and adjust trigger pull to just over 2 pounds (off the rack, it had a pull of nearly 5!), fix the feed from the magazine into the chamber (bullets frequently jammed), and I sanded and chiseled the barrel fitting in the stock so it became essentially free-floating, which dramatically improved accuracy.

Bullet Placement

Ultimately, bullet placement is far more important than caliber. Shoot for the chest cavity, for heart and lungs, on a mule deer. Unless you're close and very sure of your marksmanship under field conditions (which is quite different than shooting from a bench on a marked rifle range), ignore fancy neck and spine shots. Much of the neck is simply muscle, and a buck can go a long way with a neck shot unless you hit vertebrae, which is a small part of the neck. Ignore spine shots, too. Your chances are better shooting lower down into the chest cavity.

If a buck is broadside, shoot just behind the shoulder about 1/3 of the way between the brisket and back line. If you miss the heart, you'll get both lungs, and you'll probably get them even if you nick the heart. Lung shots are always fatal, and normally a buck running off after such a shot leaves a good blood trail. He won't go far either, rarely more than a hundred and fifty yards. The lungs occupy virtually all of the chest cavity, so if you hit higher than you'd intended, or a bit lower, or farther back, you'll still hit lungs and you'll still collect your trophy.

If the buck is facing you head-on, shoot between the shoulders; if he's quartering away, angle one in behind the rib cage so it penetrates into the chest. If the buck is close, and heading straight away, I'd try to spine him; don't shoot below the tail, however, since you'll gut-shoot him and he may get away to die miserably. If a buck is quartering toward you, aim at the point of the shoulder; here, you should break the shoulder, thereby anchoring him, and the bullet should penetrate into the chest cavity and get lungs, too. Actually, it's better to shoot a rainbow-trajectory .30/30 and be able to call your shot, than a 7mm mag with crossed fingers.

Determine Where You Hit

When field dressing, perform an autopsy to determine just where you hit, the path of the bullet, and the kind of damage your particular bullet caused. Often, you'll be able to find the bullet, and it's under the hide on the off side more than any other place. If the lead has separated from the copper jacket, the bullet isn't doing what it should. Compare the mushroomed bullet weight with the weight of an unfired bullet. A used, mushroomed bullet should lose some weight in passing through muscle and bone, but not half of it. I've found that if bullets retain 70% of their original weight they're performing adequately. If they retain more weight, they're doing well. I suspect you can get by with a bullet that retains 60% of its original weight. How much weight a particular bullet retains depends a great deal on what parts of an animal a bullet passes through; a bullet will lose more weight smashing through both shoulder blades than it will going through ribs and lungs.

When you field dress a buck, study organ placement. Note how the heart fits low in the chest, and reasonably far forward, between the lungs, and how the lungs occupy virtually all of the thoracic cavity. Note how the liver, also a fatal shot if you hit a little farther back, rests against the diaphragm almost between the posterior lobes of the lungs. Determine how the vertebrae run through the neck, in case you're forced to make a neck shot. Also determine the spine line above the thoracic and abdominal cavities, in the event you're forced to make a spine shot because the rest of the buck is hidden in brush. This knowledge allows you to better decide where to put the bullet, and bullet placement is more important than what caliber you use.

Walter "Karamojo" Bell regularly killed African elephants with small calibers, smaller even than the .270. When he killed an elephant, he autopsied it, noted bullet penetration and the location of vital organs, mainly the brain and heart. By knowing where these organs were located and what angles to shoot and hit them in various positions, he was able to kill hundreds of elephants cleanly and live to tell about it. I'm certain "Karamojo" Bell would agree that bullet placement, and knowledge of an animal's vital organs, are more important than what cartridge you use.

A perfect target!

24

Cape Care And Taxidermy

Unfortunately, too many skins and capes are ruined in the field by hunters who just don't understand the rudiments of cape care. Even guides and outfitters neglect or simply don't understand cape care. The only person that can guarantee your cape makes it to the taxidermist in good shape, is you.

Cutting Tips

A common mistake is that capes are cut too short. When removing a buck's cape (or scalp, as it's sometimes referred to), be certain you make the cuts several inches behind the shoulder (six wouldn't be too much), and that the cuts extend down to the wrist joint (some hunters call this the knee joint, though anatomically that is incorrect; in any case, it's the joint where the leg can first bend toward the posterior, and it's about midway down the leg). Of course, make the cuts upward along the back of the leg.

Slit along the back from behind the shoulder several inches, along the back of the neck nearly to the center of the base of the antlers, then make a "Y" cut, one arm of the "Y" extending to each antler. Skin carefully around the base of each antler; occasionally it's possible to work the hide free of the antler base with a screwdriver, though often you've got to use a knife. Peel the hide forward from the shoulders, along the neck toward the head. Take your time, try to remove all meat that might peel free with the hide; it's easier to do it while you're skinning than it is a day later. Go slowly, and try not to cut through the hide; cuts can be fixed, but they cost extra, and if you have too many, your trophy mount is going to look a bit shoddy. When you get to the ears, cut them off at the base, being certain not to cut through the hide at the base. You can skin them out later, after the cape is removed from the carcass; it's much easier this way.

The tough part is skinning out the face. If you're not familiar with the job, try and get it to someone who is—a taxidermist is best, or the guide or outfitter or hunting buddy. If you can't, say you're out in the bush for an extended

CAPING

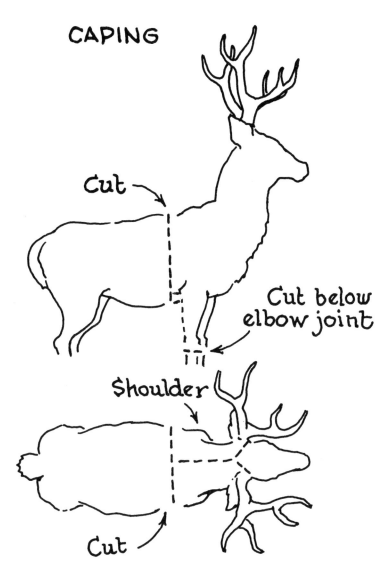

The basic cuts for removing a buck's cape.

stay or the weather is warm, then do it yourself. If you're less than comfortable doing the job, go slowly. Peel the hide away from the antlers and ear bases toward the nose, caping and fleshing very carefully as you go. Be especially cautious around the eyes and preorbital glands (the slit-like openings just in front of the eyes); I feel with a forefinger from the hair-side of the hide into the eyes (and later the nostrils, lips), and guide my fleshing from the raw side of the hide that way. Don't make a mistake here, since the hair is short on the face and it's more difficult for a taxidermist to hide any unwanted cuts through the hide. Once past the eyes, things get easy until you get to the lips and nostrils. Again, guide your cutting with a forefinger from the hair-side. Get plenty of lip material, in other words, be certain your cuts are well back from the lip tissue (later, remove most of the cartilage and fat from the inside of the lips, and what you can't remove, slit and work with salt). Get well into the nostrils, though not so far that you're removing heavy nasal cartilage with the cape. Skin slowly, and I can't emphasize this too much, especially if you're relatively inexperienced with caping. The actual caping job itself isn't that technical, and anyone can do it *if* he's cautious.

Once the cape is free of the skull, skin out the ears. This, too, can be tricky, so take your time. Peel the outside hide upward, leaving the inside cartilage attached. When you've finished, spread the entire cape out, leather side up, and remove all the fat and meat you can without cutting through to the other side. Again, take your time, and don't ruin that trophy cape.

It's critical to cool the cape quickly, and get it dry, and the sooner the better. During many early season buck hunts, the weather is warm, in which case it's vital to remove the cape immediately. If you don't, hair will begin slipping, often within hours. If there's blood on the cape, wash it off quickly, if possible, even before caping. Otherwise, I'll wash out blood as soon as the cape is free and before salting.

Salting

Once the cape is removed and clean, get it salted. Spread the cape out with the leather side up and cover it with about half an inch of salt. Work the salt into and around eyes, preorbital glands, lips and nostrils, and don't neglect the ears. Pay special attention to the edge of the cape. Let the first layer of salt stand for a day or so (remove it earlier if the cape is unusually damp from washing, or damp from weather conditions, etc.); remove the first salt layer and put on another one just as you did the first. If the weather is damp, keep the salted cape inside a tent or other shelter. Never keep the cape in a plastic bag. It can't dry if air can't get to it. Keep the leather out of direct sunlight, since ultra-violet radiation from sunlight will burn the hide. Don't store the cape near fires, heaters or other heat sources, which promote bacterial growth and hair slippage.

Avoid Drag Scars

Too many hunters also drag trophy bucks across rough ground—a critical error, since rocks, brush, blowdowns and most other things on the ground can wear off hair and damage the hide. Back in my early trophy buck hunting days, I often dragged bucks out, even big ones. In those days, I was young and tough and my youthful zeal was untempered by experience. As I write this, I have two big bucks staring down from the wall with bare drag marks on their shoulders. I bagged them back when I was in high school or just starting college, and had dragged them to the nearest Jeep trail. Fortunately, I learn from mistakes; now, I either load them on horses, game carriers, or cape the buck immediately (at least to the head) and pack out the separated trophy (cape, skull and antlers) on my back.

Strangely, hunters still cut the throat. Some cut it vertically to get the windpipe (trachea) out, and others cut it horizontally to "bleed-out" the buck. Both practices are unnecessary, so don't do them. First, removing the windpipe doesn't improve meat flavor, and doesn't do much to facilitate neck-meat cooling; when you remove the cape, the neck will cool out as quickly as it can. Second, cutting across the throat horizontally to "bleed-out" the buck doesn't do anything; the buck hemorrhages extensively where the bullet hits, normally in the body cavity, and most blood is dumped onto the ground when you gut the buck. Both practices do, however, badly ruin or damage capes. If the cape can be salvaged at all, the taxidermist will charge extra, as he should, to repair the big cuts in the hide.

Take pains with the trophy cape. Trophy mule deer are probably the toughest big game trophy in North America to collect, and I've hunted most game species. They're one of the few that really can't be bought. There are relatively few places on the continent where they have time to get old, hunter pressure isn't too heavy, there's the right genetic pool for big antlers, and there's the right soil to produce trophies. So value the trophy, take care of the cape, and pick a taxidermist that's up to the job.

Seek Qualified Taxidermy

It's a common practice, even for hunters who have just spent $60,000 on a Tanzanian safari, to try to save a few bucks on taxidermy. If you've just taken a huge mule deer buck, again, one of the toughest trophies to collect, get it done by the best. There are several international taxidermists around the country. I've had excellent results with Atcheson Taxidermy, and the owners, Tom Hardesty and Bob Meier, of Butte, Montana. They and their staff are good (they've won a number of national and international awards) and they're consistent. I would also recommend Yuri Rulin, a former Russian master taxidermist who relocated to West Jordan, Utah.

25

Deer Camps, Gear, And Miscellaneous

Not much has been written about the deer camp. To me, it's the most important part of deer hunting. If you have a pleasant, remote, properly-equipped and scenic camp, you'll have fun even if you don't shoot a buck.

Tents

Unless you're on a ranch or lodge hunt, you'll be spending time in a tent, and one that leaks or flaps to the ground each time a wind gust catches it can make a hunt miserable. Tents range in size and weight from cabin-sized A-walls to tiny, 2-pound bivvy sacks. The big A-wall tents are traditional and allow a cook stove, can seat any number of hunters around a table, and can be a place for end-of-the-day socialization. If you're hunting at the end of a 4-wheel drive trail or in the wilderness with a pack-train, my preference for the ideal camp is an A-wall tent with a good woodburning cookstove. Some tents can be pricey items, but some of the best and most reasonably priced A-wall tents are made by Kirkham's Sporting Goods of Salt Lake City (they've got a variety of sizes and models, and distribute tent stoves, too). I've used several models on deer and elk hunts, and have been satisfied with the features and durability. These tents stand up to heavy snow and strong winds if properly anchored, and they're fairly waterproof, roomy and tough.

Family-style umbrella tents are adequate for the fair weather often found in early-season hunts, but don't stand up to wind or heavy snow. They have the advantage of being inexpensive, which is why they've become popular with big-game guides in the West. A disadvantage is that you can't use a woodburning stove in them, though many guides do use gas stoves inside, which is dangerous not only because of the fire hazard but because of the fumes. I've used these tents on deer hunts, but only where I could drive to camp and only during fair weather.

167

A good deer-hunting tent for all conditions is the smaller, expedition-style tent. I have a Moss Olympia which has survived autumn squalls far north of the Arctic Circle, gale-force winds at 12,000 feet in the Canadian Rockies, and storms that dumped two feet of heavy, wet snow overnight, and yet kept me dry and comfortable. The only disadvantage is an aesthetic one, since you can't use a woodburning stove in them. (I have, however, often used small, backpacking LP stoves for cooking and heat.) Other good expedition-quality tents include some made by Marmot and North Face (the VE series), and there are a number of sizes and styles ranging from small one-man jobs up to models that can sleep ten or so. They're pricey tents, though; my Moss Olympia that will sleep 2 comfortably and three in a pinch runs over $600. I've gotten to the point that if I expect severe weather, I tote the Moss along, even on a pack-in or drive-in hunt where there's going to be an A-wall. I know the Moss will stand up to anything short of an avalanche or tornado, and if I've got it around I also know I will sleep dry and snug. I even tote it on Far North hunts where the guide is going to have a tent; I've slept in too many outfitter-furnished tents that leaked, collapsed or fell apart to trust them anymore. One example of just how tough an expedition tent is: Cheri and I were floating out from one of our then-annual eight-week backpack and float-hunt expeditions north of the Arctic Circle when a three-day blow hit. We'd camped on an exposed river bar as we floated downriver when the wind started during the night. It was a little weird, because there were no gusts and lulls, just a steady big wind in the neighborhood of 75 miles per hour, if I can make a good guess from my old ocean sailing days. It kept up for nearly three days before it began to abate. We had to anchor the tent to an immense spruce log that had washed onto the beach, but the tent held. The tent bars were permanently distorted and the rain fly had stretched a bit, but other than that, the tent held. If we'd been in an A-wall, we'd have lost the tent; an umbrella tent would have gone in the first blast.

Another kind of tent is a bivvy sack or the small backpacking tent. For solo backpack hunting, which is a good way to bag a trophy buck since most mosshorns live in remote rough country where other hunters don't go, a top-quality bivvy sack is good. The best are made by Marmot and North Face. They're light (some weigh 2 pounds), waterproof, and most "breathe" (allow body moisture to escape, usually through an inner fabric called "Gore-tex." In my experience with boots, gloves, parkas and tents, gore-tex is highly overrated, and seldom does what it's supposed to, and gore-tex items are rarely as sturdy as other gear, especially in mittens, parkas or raingear). Most bivvy sacks allow you to keep your face out in the elements if you desire, and some even have arm sleeves so you can function in the elements while remaining in your cocoon; with these, tossing a log on the fire or brewing tea is simple. The disadvantage is that you can't store gear in them and they're no fun to sit out a 3-day storm in. I use these for short trips into remote country, but if I'm going to be there a while, I use a small, light, one- or two-man tent; my favorite is the Sierra Designs "Flashlight." It weighs about 3 pounds, is reasonably sturdy (I've used it in moderate snow storms in the Arctic) and can stand up to moderate winds. It's not really designed for heavy weather camping, though. It's roomy—I can sleep comfortably, stow my gear, and even cook in it on a small backpacking LP stove. It has the advantage of being cheap, about $180 in the last store I saw it in.

Bedding

A lightweight, probably down, sleeping bag is a must in my deer hunting. I have two. One is lightweight (less than 2 pounds) which I use for backpacking where the temperature is unlikely to get below 20 degrees. It compresses into a stuff bag and takes up less space in a backpack than a miniature football; the bag is made by North Face. I have another of the same bags that I added 4 pounds more goose down to. In this bag I can sleep warmly in temperatures below zero, though it's too bulky for extended backpack hunting. If you're driving or horse-packing into camp, get something that's comfortable to you, warm, and allows movement. Here, you're not normally worried by bulk and weight, so anything can do, but for warmth I still prefer down.

When I was young, tough and foolish, I didn't worry about a sleeping pad. I unrolled my bag on the ground, and after kicking depressions for my hips and shoulders, sacked out. I was seldom comfortable, and as a result, didn't really like camping. Later, I got smart and started sleeping on pads—first on small foam pads that were better than nothing, then on small, inflatable pads. I not only didn't wake up feeling as if a mule had trampled me, but I slept warmer because I didn't lose body heat to the ground. As a result I fell in love with camping. In a pinch, a saddle blanket, clothes, game bags or tarps can serve as a cushion, but use *something*.

Clothing

I think of myself as a traditionalist; others call me old-fashioned. Either way, I prefer wool clothing for hunting. It's warm, especially if close-knitted. It's quiet when moving through brush, it wicks sweat away from the body, it's warm even when wet, and it dries quickly. It's not waterproof, however, so if you're hunting in a heavy, wet snowstorm, wear a waterproof covering over your wool, or at least several layers of wool. Synthetic pile fabrics have become popular, but I still prefer wool, mostly because I *am* old-fashioned, I guess, but also because it "breathes" better (body condensation escapes) and it's easier to dry. I do a lot of buck stalking in the woods, where I move slowly and quietly. Under these conditions, I don't have to worry about a branch scraping against wool and giving me away at a quarter of a mile. I like wool mittens, too, if it's dry. If it's not, I'll resort to gore-tex mittens with a waterproof outer.

Depending on conditions, there are a number of boot styles to choose from. Pacs (leather upper and rubber bottoms) are good for hunting in wet snow or marshy terrain; get any of a variety of models with good, aggressive tread designs so you don't slip. The best pacs are made by L.L. Bean (who invented them many years ago), Sorel from Canada, and LaCroix.

In drier conditions I use a full leather upper boot with a good, waffle-pattern vibram sole. I prefer models that reach above the ankle but no farther. That way, I get ankle support but no extra weight, and weight on feet tires a hunter more quickly than five times as much weight on the back. My favorite boots are made by Vasque, especially the Sundowner model. These are waterproof, sturdy (I'm still using the same pair I bought four years ago, and I hike pretty much nonstop from March through December, much of it in tough, rocky terrain), and light.

I won't hunt in typical rough muley country in boots that don't reach above the ankle because I find I often need that ankle support, especially when stumbling back to camp in the dark. It doesn't take an ace sleuth to know a badly-sprained ankle will ruin a deer hunt.

Packs

For backpacking, I prefer internal frame packs; they're simple, sturdy, don't catch on brush as easily as external frame packs, and keep the weight closer to the body for better balance. The one I'm using now is made by Lowe; they make a number of good models. North Face and Gregory also make good internal frame backpacks. For packing out quartered or boned-out bucks, I prefer a pack frame of some sort, especially the aluminum frames. Here, I put the weight high on the pack so I carry most of it on my shoulders instead of hips.

If I'm forced to pack a deer very far, I bone the deer out. There's no sense in packing bones and hide, and a buck will be much, much lighter without them. Simply remove the meat from the bones, put it in cheesecloth game bags, and tote it on your back. A huge buck will weight less than sixty pounds if fully boned. Boning is a simple process, requiring only a sharp knife, honing stone and common sense.

A daypack is handy when hunting all day. You can carry lunch, game bags, water, matches, honing stone, camera, raingear, a space blanket and other items which make the day and hunting more pleasant.

Camp Miscellaneous

I like to camp around water. A gurgling stream, rushing river, or lake or pond makes a campsite more fun. In addition, it's a source for drinking and washing water. I boil all water I drink, whether I'm in the Arctic wilderness or on a Wyoming ranch. Giardia organisms are common throughout mule deer county and can hospitalize a hunter. There's also numerous bacilli, protozoan and helminth parasites in water that can affect humans, so it's just safer and easier to boil water. I boil water for at least 5 minutes, which will kill even the toughest egg, cyst or spore. Chemical treatments work on some organisms but not all, and filtering enough water to keep a hunter fully hydrated is a Herculean chore.

Try to set up camp where winds aren't going to blow you off the mountain. Look at surrounding trees and brush; if they're flagged (all leaning in one direction), the place gets a lot of wind, so camp elsewhere. Don't camp under or near dead timber, since a blow might topple a ten-ton spruce snag onto camp.

Similarly, don't camp in dry ravines or arroyos, especially in arid country such as in Nevada, southern Utah, western Colorado, or much of Arizona and New Mexico. A cloudburst twenty miles away can turn a ravine into a raging torrent. I wasn't deer hunting at the time, but once in southern Utah in a ravine that drained into the Colorado River, a cloudburst in the Abajo

Mountains twenty or so miles to the east caused a flashflood where I was camping. Suddenly, in the middle of the night, a great roar filled the ravine. At dawn, I saw that the ravine was running a torrent of brown, thick water at least 6 feet deep, and the cliff a few hundred yards above had become a ninety-foot waterfall. Fortunately, I was camped above water level. Another time on a Far North moose hunt, I warned my float-hunting buddy Rick Lowe to move his raft and tent farther up the beach away from the river, since it had rained for days in the mountains to the north and I knew from past experience that the river would rise. He did, but not far enough. During the night, his raft, loaded with moose meat and gear, tore free from its mooring and floated off in the rising water, and his tent filled with water.

I like to camp on a height overlooking a canyon, so I can idly watch for deer in the canyon bottoms and opposite slope. Usually, the "edge" between an open area and a forest is a pleasant camp site, and you stand a better chance of seeing game. I feel too exposed when camping in a completely open prairie or sagebrush flat, and there's always the possibility of getting blasted by a storm.

With a little planning and thought, a deer camp can be homey. Then, not only will you enjoy hunting, you'll actually *like* to camp.

Cheri brewing campfire stew.

An A-wall tent deer camp after a heavy snow.

A completely boned-out buck ready for packing to camp.

26

Guides and Outfitters

In truth, the only times I've hunted with guides for mule deer was in Canada, as an adjunct to hunts for mountain goats, moose, and bighorn and stone sheep. Since I was an experienced trophy mule deer hunter on most of these hunts, I often knew more about getting a trophy than the guides. As far as guides in the United States go, I can't be of much help.

Nevertheless, I have used guides extensively in such places as Alberta, British Columbia, Botswana, Saskatchewan, Tanzania, Zimbabwe and other places, though not for mule deer. But what works for a guide or outfitter for mule deer applies to one for cape buffalo or stone sheep.

Most guides and outfitters are out to sell. As salesmen, many will tell you whatever will sell a hunt. In fact, some paint such a glowing picture that when you get to the area you're going to hunt, you wonder if you're in the right place. Don't hunt with a guide or outfitter that doesn't have any references, and don't spend cash on one that doesn't have at least half a dozen happy client references. Bear in mind that no guide or outfitter is going to supply you with a list of unhappy clients, and that probably there *are* some around. By talking with each client on the outfitter's list, you may be able to come up with additional names the outfitter hasn't supplied you with, and these might prove even more useful.

The first question I ask client references is whether or not the outfitter and/or guide is a trustworthy fellow. Can I believe what he tells me? Or is the outfitter/guide prone to exaggeration, or worse? If the clients all tell me he is trustworthy, then I tend to believe what the outfitter says, and I can get down to details of the hunt. Many outfitters/guides will send you photos of trophies taken in their area. Find out if these are typical heads, or rare, exceptional trophies. Find out about hunting conditions: terrain, camping areas and facilities, what kind of hunting you'll do (horseback, hiking, etc.), what kind of weather you can expect, what type of clothing and gear you should bring. If you feel you can believe what the outfitter tells you, ask about the odds for getting the trophy you want. If you're communicating with the outfitter and not the guide, ask him about the guide that will be assigned to you: is he young and overly zealous, tempered with years and experience, surly, friendly—whatever is important to you.

Try not to let your enthusiasm and hopes color your gut judgments of a guide or outfitter. You're spending a lot of wages for a hunt, you want an exceptional trophy, so be practical, and judge the outfitter first. If you have a gut reaction against the guy, maybe you should trust that, but find out specifics and check with references just the same, in case your gut feelings are wrong. A lot of guides and some outfitters, especially in North America, have gone into guiding simply because they don't have other work at that time of year. A blanket statement like that is somewhat unfair to some good and hard-working guides and outfitters, but the statement is true, just the same. In North America, the best guides tend to come from western Canada, and the very best are African professional hunters who hunt six or more months of the year and consider guiding a profession, not a sideline until they can get back to jobs on the ranch or oil field.

Over the past decade I've polled my hunting chums about guides and outfitters. The results say the worst come from Alaska, possibly because the economy in Alaska is terribly depressed, there are few if any unskilled jobs, and every young male that has hunted a moose seeks an apprentice guide job in the autumn. The pay is terrible, but better than nothing, for apprentice and even registered guides working for a master guide/outfitter, so the job isn't going to attract the higher quality people that become professional hunters in Africa. Since this book is about mule deer hunting, we don't need to worry much about Alaska, unless you plan to hunt the tiny coastal deer there. I lived in Alaska for a dozen years, had neighbors that worked as guides in hunting season and scrounged the rest of the year, but have never hunted with an Alaskan guide. Most of the guides I did know, however, were pretty motorized, and if you couldn't get there with an ATV, powerboat, half-track or chartered bush plane, they were helpless. In addition, there's been a lot of illegal recent activity involving guides and outfitters, and if your guide is doing something illegal and you don't know it, you're just as liable as he is. Fish and Wildlife Protection state troopers have been involved in some of the illegal activity as well as biologists. The laws are tough in Alaska, very confusing, and in some cases, contradictory, so steer clear unless you're sure of your guide.

In addition to Canada, western Wyoming produces some good mule deer guides. There are also some good ones operating in wilderness areas of Idaho and Montana. Ranch guides tend to be ranchers or hired hands first, and hunting guides second or third.

Guides are not a necessity for mule deer hunting, even trophy buck stalking. If a hunter from the East or West coast does his homework, he can make a hunt on his own, and if he gets a trophy buck, it will mean more than if someone did everything but pull the trigger for him. If you're planning a hunt, get BLM and USFS topographical maps and check areas where big bucks have been taken (from record books); check with outfitters and guides as a potential client (though this is a bit sneaky); phone local taxidermists and find out the size and places where good bucks have been taken. Many ranches offer self-guided hunts and many contain some good bucks, particularly in Wyoming. Some operate on a trophy-fee basis; kill a big buck and you pay X, and if you get a smaller one, you don't pay as much. This is a good way into do-it-yourself trophy buck hunting.

But if you're using a guide, investigate thoroughly, and if you're going to spend all those wages, remember that the biggest bucks need time to grow to trophy proportions and they're more likely to get that size in remote wilderness areas. There, even if you don't get a buck, you'll see pristine wild country, have an exciting adventure, learn outdoor skills, and have a good time, all of which are just as important as pulling the trigger.

Again, I haven't hunted with the following outfitter, but I have talked with him in person, and I know several people who have hunted with him. From everything I can learn, this outfitter is as near as you can come to a safe wager on a trophy mule deer outfitter:

> Carlos G. Hermosillo
> Big Game Outfitters Mexico   Phone (525) 671-2064
> Sausales 44   FAX (525) 671-2207
> Mexico, 14330, D.F.

Hermosillo hunts in Sonora, in northwestern Mexico, and his clients have taken some remarkable heads, several over 40 inches in spread.

Modern results also show the Campillo brothers of Sonora are collecting some huge bucks, and most hunters I've talked with are happy with their hunts. Larry Richards, hunting in western Wyoming and wilderness Idaho, is also collecting some very good trophies; he's productive, if a bit intense.

Index

Escape, 70, 120
  Feeding, 69
  Migration, 69
  Trails, 70
Expedition-style tent, 168
External frame packs, 170
Extreme cold, 95
Eyesight, 16

F

Fawn's birth, 17
Feed plants, 144
Feeding
  Areas, 73
  Trails, 69
Field & Stream, 155
Field dressing, 159
Fighting, 118
Fleshing, 164
Float
  Hunting, 136
  Facts, 137
Floating
  For river-bottom bucks, 133
  Early, 137
  Late, 137
Fog, 93
Foods, preferred, 18

G

Galloping, 76
"Get a .270", 155
Guides, 174
Gun, 155

T